TRADITIONS AND VALUES

American Diplomacy, 1790 - 1865

Edited by

Norman A. Graebner

Series Editor
Kenneth W. Thompson

UNIVERSITY
PRESS OF
AMERICA

LANHAM • NEW YORK • LONDON

Library of Congress Cataloging in Publication Data
Main entry under title:

Traditions and values.

(American values projected abroad ; v. 7)
"Co-published by arrangement with the White
Burkett Miller Center of Public Affairs, University of
Virginia"—Verso of t.p.
Includes bibliographies.
1. United States—Foreign relations—1783-1865—
Addresses, essays, lectures. I. Graebner, Norman A.
II. Series.
JX1417.A74   1982 vol. 7   303.4'8273 s   85-7334
[E183.7]   [327.73]
ISBN 0-8191-4388-X (alk. paper)
ISBN 0-8191-4389-8 (pbk. : alk. paper)

AMERICAN VALUES PROJECTED ABROAD

VOLUME VII

A SERIES FUNDED BY THE
EXXON EDUCATION FOUNDATION

FOUNDATIONS OF AMERICAN VALUES

AMERICAN VALUES VIEWED THROUGH OTHER CULTURES

TABLE OF CONTENTS

PREFACE

With this volume conceived and organized by the distinguished American historian, Norman H. Graebner, the Miller Center of Public Affairs will publish a set of three volumes on American diplomacy. It would be inconceivable to exclude American diplomacy from a series on American values projected abroad. The first task of diplomacy is to achieve communication and dialogue among nations of widely divergent cultures and values. Moreover, a tradition of values and operative principles informs and inspires American diplomacy, however slight the understanding of some political appointees may be.

We propose, therefore, to study that tradition in three distinct historical periods: 1790-1865, 1865-1945 and 1945-1982. The first period constitutes the subject matter of this volume, the seventh volume in the Exxon Series. Professor Graebner who holds the Randolph P. Compton chair has enlisted the help of some of the nation's première authorities writing on our earliest national leaders. Graebner's own writings, his unrivaled success as a professor and his standing as a world class historian taken together assure the excellence of the pages that follow.

Kenneth W. Thompson

INTRODUCTION

The modern world consists of an increasing number of individual sovereign states suspended in a fundamentally anarchical world. Each country confronts the necessity of discovering the rules of international behavior that will not only permit it to live in an environment of maximum peace and security but also to behave in a manner that will assure the continuance of that order until some new arrangement, presumably better, can replace it. The modern state system was a creation of the international politics of the seventeenth and eighteenth centuries. It evolved from necessity as a number of powerful and sometimes ambitious nations, living under no law but their own, attempted to guarantee their economic and political independence from the aggressions of neighboring rulers. Ultimately the modern state system found the necessary guarantees of existence in the balance of power which rested on the assumption that preponderant power at any given moment preferred the existing arrangement, with its individual sovereignties, to the destruction of the established order. Assuming that every nation played an essential role in the international equilibrium, the balancing system sought to defend the independent existence of the weak as well as the strong from the power of others. The system was never designed to eliminate war but merely to minimize its consequences, leaving each nation intact. Nowhere in the system was there any mechanism whereby rulers could drive aggression from the international scene; thus there would be wars. What preserved the system was the capacity of states which favored the status quo over change to limit the ambitions of aggressors either by encouraging moderation under the threat of countering violence or by actually defeating them in war. In its defense of the status quo, defined broadly enough to accommodate the incontrovertable shifts in power and interest, the balancing system worked. Not one European aggressor of modern times possessed the ultimate power to triumph over its enemies and thus redesign the map of Europe. When occasionally a country disappeared, as did Poland in the eighteenth century, it was because the major powers agreed that such elimination would strengthen rather than weaken the international equilibrium. It was into this world of power politics that the United States was born.

Within the new Republic the highly emotional and exhilerating experience of the Revolution created two distinct sets of values to govern the external relations of the nation, and thereby define its proper relationship to the existing international order. One partook of the realization that the American people, through their successful revolt against Great Britain, had established the foundations of the modern world's first experiment in republican government. Indeed, the American Revolution had created a model for the world to follow. The notions of society embodied in Revolutionary thought reflected a deep faith in reason and progress, even in the perfectibility of human society. For many of its adherents the American Revolution was designed to encourage other revolutions, ultimately toppling kings and despots everywhere who held power at the expense of humane values. In its attack on the alleged tyranny of King George III the Declaration of Independence proclaimed principles of government that appeared applicable to all who struggled against monarchy and autocracy. Benjamin Franklin acknowledged such sentiments when he wrote in 1782: "Establishing the liberties of America will not only make the people happy, but will have some effect in diminishing the misery of those, who in other parts of the world groan under despotism, by rendering it more circumspect, and inducing it to govern with a lighter hand." For those who accepted the obligation to embody such universalistic notions in American foreign policy the country would of necessity make distinctions among nations, not on the basis of their relationship to this nation's economic and security interests, but on the basis of their forms of government and their behavior toward their subjects.

Those who opposed this ideological approach to the country's external relations preferred the more traditional and, for the country's early leaders the infinitely more acceptable, view that the United States not only existed in a world of power politics, but also that in its willingness to understand and practice the rules imposed by that world lay the surest protection of its own interests, security, and continued independence. The Revolutionary generation knew that its astonishing successes as it acted on the international stage over the previous three decades had rested on the existence of the European balance of power, with Britain and France constituting the two poles of that balancing structure. This permitted the early leaders to draw on British power to remove the French from the North American continent in the Seven Years' War (1756–1763). During subsequent years that same Anglo-French rivalry, the central element in Europe's equilibrium, permitted them to secure needed French support in their long and successful war against England. With good reason the Revolutionary leaders accepted the European state system as a fundamental and welcome necessity. John Adams instructed James Warren how the balance of power system had protected the United States in its struggle for independence:

> [T]here is a Ballance of Power in Europe. Nature has formed it. Practice and Habit have confirmed it, and it must forever exist. It may be disturbed for a time, by the accidental Removal of a Weight from one Scale to the other; but there will be a continual Effort to restore the Equilibrium. The Powers of Europe now think Great Britain too powerful. They will see her Power diminished with pleasure. But they cannot see Us throw ourselves headlong into the Scale of Bourbon [power] without Jealousy and Terror. We must therefore give no exclusive priviledges in Trade to the House of Bourbon. If We give exclusive priviledges in Trade, or form perpetual Alliances offensive and defensive with the Powers in one Scale, We infallibly make Enemies of those in the other, and some of these at least will declare War in favor of Great Britain. Congress adopted these Principles and this System in its purity, and by their Wisdom have succeeded most perfectly in preventing every Power in the World from taking Part against them.

With the treaty of 1783 the Founding Fathers understood that American independence rested on the continued rivalry of France and Great Britain, with each nation denying the other the freedom and the authority to infringe on the settlement that granted the United States its independence.

Of the European writers who had defined the European state system and had extracted from Europe's experience the rules that enabled the system to function, none impressed the early Americans more than Emmerich de Vattel who published his *Law of Nations* in 1758. All the Founding Fathers had read and imbibed the precepts of Vattel, but especially Alexander Hamilton. Thus the opening essay in this volume comprises the necessary bridge from the European system and those who analyzed it to the embodiment of that system's principles in the foreign policies of the Washington administration. That administration, largely through Hamilton's leadership, sought to make the young Republic not only a nation among nations as a reality but also as a performing member of an established system, conducting its external relations by the rules of that system. Hamilton's writings, especially his "Pacificus" and "Americanus" papers of 1793 and 1794, comprise one long and brilliant commentary on Vattel, applied specifically to the needs and challenges of the United States created by the wars of the French Revolution.

Subsequent designers of American foreign policy, especially that small group of Revolutionary leaders and those—John Quincy Adams, Daniel Webster, and William H. Seward—who claimed to be their intellectual successors, understood the international system well. They agreed in general on the role that the United States should play in that system. Jefferson and Madison knew their Vattel, although they, with Monroe, at times departed from Vattel's teachings in their reversion to a more sentimental, ideological view of the country's foreign relations. But John Quincy Adams, as Monroe's secretary of state, exemplified the precepts of Washington and Hamilton in pure form. Daniel Webster, if less a theoretician than Adams, appreciated the country's early diplomatists and applied their principles elegantly, as indeed did William H. Seward, the last subject of this volume. The seven early builders of this country's foreign policies, whose careers, intellectually and practically, comprise the subject matter of this book, established a tradition that was at once realistic, mindful of the nation's interests as well as its limited power, and generally understood if not always appreciated by the world's major powers. As such these seven men merit the attention and the understanding of all Americans. Leaders no more than citizens can profitably hold views regarding foreign affairs that are divorced from the country's early traditions and values, especially because those traditions and values conformed to the realities of a world of sovereign states—realities that persist in the twentieth century—and because they served this nation well.

1

ALEXANDER HAMILTON AND THE LAW OF NATIONS

Daniel Lang

As the bicentennial celebration of the Constitution of the United States approaches, Americans again have occasion to consider and to applaud the work of those who established the new government and successfully guided the young Republic through a turbulent period of international relations. Some of that early diplomatic success may be attributed to the wealth of experience abroad that leaders such as Thomas Jefferson, Benjamin Franklin, John Adams, and John Jay brought to the emerging nation. The most influential figure in shaping American foreign policy in the 1790s, however, was Alexander Hamilton. Hamilton brought into national life not a long diplomatic experience but a strong sense for the fundamentals of a problem, formidable powers of reasoning, and a sure understanding of international politics and law.

American leaders in the late eighteenth century were as familiar with the new science of international politics and law which had emerged with the Enlightenment as they were aware of the impact of European politics on their own lives. Among their teachers were the political theorists David Hume, Baron Montesquieu, and John Locke, the polemicist Charles Davenant, and writers on the law of nations Hugo Grotius and Emmerich de Vattel. In defending their policies, they came to rely especially on Vattel's *Law of Nations,* first published in 1758. Historian Charles Fenwick has written that "not even the name of Grotius himself was more potent in its influence upon questions relating to international law than that of

1

Vattel."[1] In 1775 Benjamin Franklin thanked a friend for sending him several copies of Vattel's work and added:

> I am much obliged by the kind present you have made us of your edition of Vattel. It came to us in good season, when the circumstances of a rising State make it necessary frequently to consult the Law of Nations. Accordingly, that copy which I kept ... has been continually in the hands of members of our Congress now sitting.[2]

Thomas Jefferson held Vattel in high esteem. When he remonstrated formally to Citizen Genet about his conduct and claims, he found his needed authority there:

> We are of opinion it [United States policy] is dictated by the law of nature and the usage of nations; and this has been very materially inquired into before it was adopted as a principle of conduct. But we will not assume the exclusive right of saying what that law and usage is. Let us appeal to enlightened and disinterested judges. None is more so than Vattel.[3]

Alexander Hamilton referred to Vattel as "perhaps the most accurate and approved of the writers on the laws of Nations" and regularly invoked his authority in cabinet opinions and public defenses of administration policy. Hamilton frequently cited Vattel on specific issues—the rights of neutrals, the treatment of alien private property during war, the treatment of prisoners of war, treaty obligations. and the rights of free passage—and the structure of his reasoning in foreign policy reflected an understanding of Vattel's treatment of the new science of international law and politics.[4] This essay will discuss the principles of that science and then reveal how those principles shaped Hamilton's views.

The modern science of international law and politics emerged in the sixteenth and seventeenth centuries in reaction to both the destructiveness of the wars of religion and the danger of universal monarchy or world empire. Revulsion against the former led to the formulation of a secular law of nature and law of nations; fear of the latter led to the idea of the balance of power. These two responses tended to reinforce one other in the eighteenth century as the European states began to reconcile themselves to one another's existence within a framework of equilibrium grounded in commonly accepted nonecclesiastical principles of legitimacy, underwritten by the law of nature and nations.

Francisco de Vitoria, who published a major work on international law in 1532, and Grotius, who wrote a century later, had prepared the way for such a grounding by interpreting the medieval just-war tradition as primarily natural rather than divine. Their understanding of natural law, however, remained heavily classical, resting on the rational and social nature of man. While each sought to minimize or eliminate the resort to war for religious purposes, both retained the notion of punitive war, because natural law applied directly to individuals and to states and sanctioned the use of force.[5]

The rise of absolutist monarchies and the emergence of the European balance of power system, recognized by the Treaty of Westphalia in 1648, encouraged a new and self-consciously modern account of political practice. The balance of power, David Hume contended in his famous *Political Discourses* (1752), was, as system and as policy, "a secret in politics, fully known only in the present age."[6] Equally modern was the doctrine of sovereignty developed by Thomas Hobbes in *Leviathan* (1651), and it was to his work that writers on the law of nations increasingly turned. In Hobbes, said Vattel, "we discover the hand of a master, notwithstanding his paradoxes and detestable maxims."[7] By using social contract arguments Vattel sought to rationalize, legitimize, and ameliorate the actual practice of states in the European system.

The states of modern Europe were above all independent. They recognized no authority above their own, defined their own interests and pursued them. Vattel argued that with certain modifications this was right and proper. Like many of Hobbes' successors, Vattel softened Hobbes' brutal account of human nature while retaining his doctrine of sovereignty. Even in the state of nature one would find "social" passions and a kind of society among men, which provided the basis for the law of nature and the existence of certain reciprocal rights and duties among men.[8] This natural sociability was not strong enough, however, to overcome disorderly passions and private or mistaken interest and so men had recourse to political association as "the only means of securing the condition of the good, and repressing the wicked; and the law of nature itself approves this establishment."[9] Since the individual state was the primary, if not the only, agent for securing individual wants, its principal duty was to itself and to its members. This meant an inherent right to self-defense and to "every thing that can secure it from . . . a threatening danger."[10]

The law of nature, which mandated a duty to help others, applied to states as well as to individuals. Because of the unique character of the state, Vattel argued that the law of nature applied differently to states. The duties of a nation to itself required more circumspection and care than those of an individual to himself. As Hamilton would put it in his "Pacificus" letters, "the duty of making its own welfare the guide of its actions is much stronger upon states than upon individuals."[11] The sovereign rights of others further circumscribed this duty because one state could not be the judge of what was best for another:

> It is an evident consequence of the liberty and indepen-
> dence of nations that all have a right to be governed as
> they think proper and that no state has the smallest
> right to interfere in the government of another.[12]

When applied to states, then, the law of nature tended to define virtue as non-interference; or, as Vattel formulated the second law of nations: "each nation should be left in the peaceable enjoyment of the liberty which she inherits from nature."[13]

Several consequences important to the early Americans followed from this emphasis on the rights of sovereignty in the law of nations: it provided the underpinnings for a policy of neutrality in war, it established the basis for the separation of moral and legal obligations or what Vattel termed the "necessary" and the "voluntary" law of nations, and it permitted a distinction between external liberty (independence) and internal liberty (republicanism).[14]

The relative self-sufficiency of the state also meant that political association between nations was much less necessary than association between individuals. The law of nature did not require world government, as some of Vattel's predecessors had suggested. What impressed Vattel about Europe was its cultural unity and its political diversity. Modern Europe had become "a kind of republic, of which the members—each independent, but all linked together by the ties of common interest—unite for the maintenance of order and liberty."[15]

II

For Vattel, the key to order and liberty in Europe was "the famous scheme of the political balance, or the equilibrium of power, by which is understood such a disposition of things, as that no one potentate be able absolutely to predominate, and prescribe laws to others."[16] The law of nations reflected the balance of power structure and was in turn thought to sustain the essential elements of the European system. The incorporation of the theory of sovereignty into the law of nations provided a basis in right for the fundamental aim of the balance of power system, namely the assurance of the survival of independent states.[17] Americans understood this. During the Constitutional debates James Madison and Hamilton sought to allay the fears of small state advocates by arguing that the large states would counter each other rather than act in concert, thereby preserving the whole and indirectly protecting the small states from domination. In Madison's words:

> Among individuals of superior eminence and weight in society, rivalships were much more frequent than coalitions. Among independent nations preeminent over their neighbors, the same remark was verified. Carthage and Rome tore one another to pieces instead of uniting their forces to devour the weaker nations of the earth. The Houses of Austria and France were hostile as long as they remained the greatest powers of Europe. England and France have succeeded to the preeminence and to the enmity. To this principle we owe perhaps our liberty. . . . [18]

The new science identified the alternative to individual, competing states—universal monarchy—with world tyranny. An arrangement based on the existence of several independent loci of power and authority, though it could not ensure peace, still presented fewer evils. Hume wrote fearfully of the consequences of universal monarchy where a a powerful monarch, imbued with religious zeal, would seek to oppress the world.[19] The balance of power system presented the possibility that at least some of humankind could experience a modicum of security and comfort; it also meant that there would be a safe haven in other states for those fleeing persecution in their own.[20]

Formal commitment by sovereign equals in a society of states to respect one another's equality tended to increase the stability of the system, as did adherence to a common set of ideas about the rules of conduct for states in the system.[21] The fact that *all* states possessed the same right to self-preservation and self-perfection limited the extent to which these rights could be invoked. The attempt of one to usurp the rights of another gave the latter the right to punish the former and secure reparation. The law of nations also justified many (although certainly not all) of the practical workings of the balance of power system, especially the making of treaties, formation of alliances and confederations, resort to war, and the pursuit of limited aims with limited means.

As explicated by Vattel, the law of nations ruled out religious war, war for universal empire, and barbaric war. On the first point, for example, Vattel argued that a nation could not force its humanitarianism on another state because to do so would be to violate that state's sovereignty or natural liberty. Thus he rejected Spain's claim that it had a right to its American colonies on the basis of a civilizing or Christianizing duty; he maintained that Spain had violated the Indians' natural rights.[22] The voluntary law taught states which were not party to a war to regard both sides as equally just, at least with respect to their external behavior. This law also extended to the attitude of foreign officials to tyrannical states. As contemporary just-war theorist Michael Walzer puts it, "foreign officials must act as if [tyrannical states are] legitimate, that is, must not make war against them."[23] As a rule, then, the internal character of another regime is unacceptable as a basis for a justifiable foreign policy. This rule reflected a fundamental quality of the European system, epitomized by Cardinal Richelieu's alliance with the German Protestants against Spain. Statesmen made alliances with other states irrespective of the internal character of those other states.

One of the charges which Hamilton would make about the French Revolutionaries was that they had violated this norm. By declaring that France would defend citizens "vexed for the cause of liberty" in every country, France had invited sedition throughout Europe. In Hamilton's view,

> To assist a people in a reasonable and virtuous struggle
> for liberty, already begun, is both justifiable and laudable;
> but to incite to revolution every where, by indiscrimi-
> nately making offers of assistance before hand, it to in-
> vade and endanger the foundations of social tranquility.[24]

Intervention in civil war, like the establishment of spheres of influence, was one instrument in the balance of power system. Yet frequent resort to such intervention would undermine the moderation which such a system was expected to promote and would cast doubt on the reality of sovereignty, which was the moral and legal cornerstone on which the system rested.[25]

On the second point, repudiation of war for world empire, the obvious ground was self-defense; but what of indirect threats or threats to the system itself? If a ruler could go to the defense of a state unjustly attacked by a powerful enemy without exposing himself to great danger, he ought to do it even though no formal obligation bound him to such a course. In advising this course of action Vattel implicitly defended the operation of the European balance of power system as productive of the good of all. He cited with approval the example of the alliance formed to prevent Louis XIV from taking the Netherlands and the decision of the King of Poland who saved Austria, possibly Germany, and even his own country by turning back the Turks who had laid seige to Vienna.[26] Duty, i.e. the obligation to assist others, coincided here with the sovereign's own interest because it "may be his own case to stand in need of assistance; and consequently, he is acting for the safety of his own nation in giving energy to the spirit and disposition to afford mutual aid."[27] In helping to preserve the fabric of international society, he was preserving his part as well. Vattel heartily endorsed the formation of alliances or confederacies which would oppose any formidable power which gave evidence of its intention to dominate Europe.[28] Such action was legitimate because of the threat to the perfect rights of other European sovereign states. It was even permissible to counter the weight of a powerful state which "by the justice and circumspection of her conduct, affords us no room to take exception to her proceedings."[29]

Finally, the law of nations sought to encourage moderation in the conduct of war, by repudiating barbaric war. Removing religion-based resorts to force was an important step in that direction, and Vattel emphasized that because one's enemies are also men, one should employ the minimum amount of force necessary to bring them to reason. He rejected needless violence directed at the lands and cities of the enemy and encouraged the maintenance of older notions of noncombatancy. In part, this reflected an appreciation for the fact that outrageous conduct in war can often perpetuate the dangers to civilization.

The operation of the European system provided incentives for states to exercise the kind of moderation which the law of nations taught. The realization by statesmen that attempts to overturn the system would probably fail encouraged them to seek essentially marginal advantages rather than outright control of other states. Political leaders preferred restraint in victory rather than unconditional surrender because today's enemy could well be needed as tomorrow's ally and today's ally could well become tomorrow's adversary.[30]

To focus on marginal advantages was to seek mundane, limited objectives such as security, wealth, or territory. It would make little sense for an army invading to possess a rich province to devastate the province and destroy what made it desirable in the first place. Limitations of power and wealth made sovereigns acutely aware of the need to weigh the costs and the benefits of waging war. Within the broad limits which helped to define moderation Vattel left it to the various sovereigns to define for themselves the justice of their case. This sustained the possibility that his doctrine might sanction wars which he actually would have regarded as unjust, but which would still be moderate because of their moderate aims.

Even if the sovereign was reasonably confident that he had a just cause, he must also consider the benefits war might bring to his state; these benefits appeared in the context of the proper motives for war. Vattel like Grotius and others before him urged in his just-war theory the criterion of a cost-benefit calculation which was to him the core of prudence:

> [I]n order to be justifiable in taking up arms it is necessary — 1. That we have a just cause for complaint. 2. That a reasonable satisfaction has been denied us. 3. The ruler of the nation, as we have observed, ought maturely to consider whether it be for the advantage of the state to prosecute its right by force of arms.[31]

This held true for prospective allies as well:

> If there be question of contracting an alliance with a nation already engaged in a war, or on the point of engaging in one, two things are to be consulted: 1. The justice of that nation's quarrel. 2. The welfare of the state.[32]

Indeed, on the second point Vattel indicated that inability or possible self-destruction negated treaty obligations, as did an ally's folly or injustice. The idea of proportionality in considering the resort to war required contemplation of the war's impact upon one's own society and the interest of the society the war was intended to serve.

The outbreak of the French Revolution and the subsequent course of the French Republic challenged or ignored many of the constraints which had been an accepted part of the European system. Inevitably the conflict injected itself into American politics and provided the context in which debates about American foreign policy in the 1790's took place.

III

As President Washington's second term of office began in the spring of 1793, he and his administration faced the problem of impending war in Europe perpetrated by the French Revolution. Austria and Prussia had formed an alliance against France, Spain was already moving against France, and it seemed more and more probable that Great Britain would be drawn into the contest as well. The Americans realized that war between France and Great Britain would have serious ramifications for American policy and commerce; Great Britain in particular, with her powerful navy, her commercial dominance, and her position in British North America posed a potential threat to American security. When war actually broke out, Washington's cabinet issued a proclamation designed to keep American citizens from involving themselves in the hostilities. Cabinet agreement on that course did not extend, however, to the meaning of neutrality, which in turn reflected different strategic approaches, different estimates of the distribution of power and different assessments of the possibilities of the law of nations.

One approach, favored by Thomas Jefferson and James Madison, took as its model the successful American Revolutionary War, where the French and Spanish counterweight to British power had provided the basis for American independence. Advocates of this approach believed that the greatest threat to American interests and security came from the British; therefore, they argued, the United States ought to maintain its ties with France to counter British power and moderate British practice in trade, navigation, and belligerent rights. Jefferson and Madison understood the link between the law of nations and the distribution of power: since the law of nations pertaining to trade and neutral rights largely reflected British dominance of the seas, a shift in the distribution of power was necessary for a change in the law of nations more favorable to American interests. Moreover, they believed that the United States as a supplier of raw materials could expect the Europeans to offer much for the "necessaries" of life. On the question of the war in Europe, then, they noted the desirability of remaining at peace with the warring parties and urged a policy of "fair neutrality," but one which did not renounce American ties with France in the 1778 treaties of alliance and commerce nor continued use of the French

9

alliance as a counterweight to British power.[33]

Hamilton, on the other hand, believed that it was imperative for the United States to avoid giving unnecessary offense to Britain, especially in light of manifold American weaknesses. There were, moreover, additional reasons not to offend the British. The effort throughout the 1780's to build up American trade with France to counter the British monopoly of trade had done little to alter the American preference for British goods. Instead of undermining British trade by adopting a pro-French course, Hamilton sought to exploit that trade as a source of revenue for the new government and as a pool of investment on which to build a national economy. Finally, as Hamilton made clear in his Nootka Sound Opinion (1790), the United States had a right to the navigation of the Mississippi and an interest in gaining the port of New Orleans from the Spanish. This object, which he rated even higher than the return of the British-held forts along the Canadian border, might require war. In a possible war with Spain, the United States would naturally seek aid from Great Britain; consequently "we may have a more urgent interest to differ with Spain, than with Britain."[34] The Hamiltonian commitment to avoid antagonizing the British had to conflict at some point with the spirit, if not the letter, of the 1778 treaties. To Jeffersonians, this was a policy of unnecessary appeasement of British imperialism, particularly because it drew back from the attempt to challenge British power and the effort to obtain British concessions on navigation and belligerent rights.

Hamilton saw the unsettled political situation in 1793 in France and Europe as an opportunity to suspend the French treaties at least until a legitimate government had been established. Neutrality had been the great desideratum of American foreign policy from the early days of the Revolution. Although necessity had compelled the Americans to draw up an alliance with France, American statesmen generally understood the wisest course for the nation was that of remaining as little entangled as possible in the policies and controversies of the European states.[35] Hamilton, in his cabinet paper on the Nootka Sound question, reiterated the point that the soundest policy for the United States was "to steer as clear as possible of all foreign connection, other than commercial, and in this respect to cultivate intercourse with all the world on the broadest basis of reciprocal privilege."[36] However, with the possibility of general war in Europe, the treaties with France could jeopardize the neutrality and freedom of action which Hamilton sought for the United States; it was this problem that the European crisis raised in the deepest way.

In addition, Hamilton decided very quickly that the course the French Republic had set for itself in 1792 and 1793 fundamentally threatened the European balance of power system. Hamilton's quickness to judge was no doubt affected by domestic considerations and the threat to his financial system which a French-oriented neutrality would have entailed,[37] but also inherent in Hamilton's judgment was his understanding of the balance of power system and the just-war theory laid out by Vattel.

The uproar caused by the Proclamation of Neutrality, which went contrary to the sentiments of Americans who sympathized with France against Britain, compelled Hamilton to defend the administration's policy publicly. The result was the series of papers signed "Pacificus" in 1793 and "Americanus" in 1794. These efforts would later be followed by the papers signed "Camillus" in 1795 defending the Jay Treaty and "The Stand" in 1798 advocating war with France. In each of these there were extensive references to the law of nations and many citation, to the approved writers on the subject. Such references were fewest in "The Stand," but there the controlling concern was the threat of universal empire from France, a threat which Vattel taught was just cause for war. In each set of papers Hamilton treated first the issues of rights and the law of nations, then put forth some strategic view, and finally offered a course of action. This order strongly resembled that established by Vattel where he spoke first of "justificatory rights," then of "motives" or interests, and finally of prudence or proportionality as a means-ends calculation.

As Pacificus, Hamilton, relying largely on the authority of Vattel, stressed the distinction between offensive and defensive wars to insist that the treaties with France were defensive in nature and hence inapplicable in this situation. Central to Hamilton's reasoning was Vattel's distinction between legal or positive right (the voluntary law of nations) and moral right (the necessary law of nations). The terms offensive and defensive merely indicated who attacked first: "the cause or occasion of the war and the war itself are things entirely distinct. Tis the commencement of the war itself that decides the question of being on the offensive or defensive."[38] France's declaration of war and initiation of hostilities clearly made her the offensive party whatever the merits of her cause. This rendered the treaty with France inapplicable. For the United States the only question that mattered was who began the war; this followed from the duties of the United States under the voluntary law of nations:

> When a war breaks out between two nations, all other nations, in regard to the positive rights of the parties and their positive duties towards them are bound to consider it as equally just on both sides.[39]

For Hamilton to say that France was the offensive power in the war was not to say that France was the unjust power (though Hamilton would suggest that too). This concise summary of the voluntary law of nations alone would have been sufficient grounds for non-execution of the treaty. Because the French treaties were explicitly defensive, the United States had no legal obligation to fulfill. Nevertheless the necessary law of nations required that there also be consideration of the justness of France's war aims and the means it employed to achieve them.

IV

In arguing that France was the unjust power, Hamilton pointed to (a) the French threat to the balance of power system, (b) French violations of her treaty obligations, (c) French declarations of opposition to monarchical principles, which made France an enemy to all monarchies and which violated the norm of non-criticism of the regimes of one's neighbors, and (d) unjust French conduct in prosecuting its war. Like the authorities on which he drew, Hamilton located the basis for the maintenance of the balance of power system within the law of nations. This made a threat to the system by one power seeking dominance punishable by the other nations in the name of the law of nations. Thus he treated a threat to one nation as a threat to the others:

> There is no principle better supported by the doctrines of writers, the practice of nations, and the dictates of right reason, than this—that whenever a nation adopts maxims of conduct tending to the disturbance of the tranquility and established order of its neighbors, or manifesting a spirit of self-aggrandisement—it is lawful for other nations to combine against it, and, by force, to control the effects of those maxims and that spirit. The conduct of France, in instances which have been stated, calmly and impartially viewed, was an offence against the law of nations, which naturally made in a common cause among them to check her career.[40]

One indication of French intentions was the way France had disregarded her treaty obligations. By violating her treaty with Holland on navigation rights, by taking steps to re-open Antwerp, which the British had closed by treaty, and by incorporating territories taken by arms rather than holding them as bargaining chips for a future peace, France had taken up arms against the law of nations. This renunciation by France of its formal treaty obligations could legitimately be regarded as just cause for war by those arrayed against France. Britain could plausibly claim that it was acting on the conviction that, as W. Allison Phillips has written, "it was incumbent upon her to champion established rights, guaranteed by the public law of Europe, against a power for which neither established rights nor international law had any validity."[41] For Hamilton, French actions showed an intention to build a continental empire which threatened the European system.

Equally unsettling was the attack by France on monarchical principles which sustained many of the European states. French statements that France would defend all the friends of republican principles seemed to re-create a Europe torn by religious strife where the principles of internal rule came under the scrutiny of other states. As explicated by Vattel, the law of nations was the application of the law of nature to sovereign states; its focus was on external, not internal, liberty. This rule was one which Hamilton charged that the French had violated:

> The pretext of propagating liberty can make no difference. Every nation has a right to carve out its own happiness in its own way, and it is the height of presumption in another to attempt to fashion its political creed.[42]

As Hamilton saw it, the justice of the war on France's side was "not a little problematical." This was true in spite of French claims that its cause was the cause of liberty. In the French Convention of 1792 Revolutionary France challenged all Europe in saying that she would grant fraternity and assistance to every people who should desire to recover their liberty. Hamilton called himself a friend of liberty, but not when the cause of liberty amounted to nothing more than interference by one nation in the internal government of another. In finding France's case morally as well as legally questionable, Hamilton did not mean to enlist the United States on the side of Britain against France; he intended rather to

13

show the ambiguity of the French claim to justice, thereby releasing the United States of any moral obligation. As for the moral obligation against France (politically impossible in any case) Hamilton remarked, "I have no where found it maintained that the justice of a war is a consideration which can oblige a nation to do what its formal obligations do not require."[43] That was a consideration in the realm of imperfect rights and duties, where nations could elect to help others but were not formally required to do so.

Having considered the legal and the moral case for France, Hamilton turned to the political or prudential case. The essential criteria here were the prospects of success and the weighing of potential advantages against potential "mischiefs and perils" for the United States. With most of Europe, particularly the maritime powers, ranged against France, and with the United States "wholly destitute of naval force," it was unlikely that the United States could offer much material support and would certainly find "the most calamitous inconveniences" to its trade if it joined France. This disproportion in itself would have rendered the treaty obligation invalid: good faith did not require that the United States hazard its very existence to secure France her American possessions (as the treaty provided). France's intemperance had led her to her predicament and Americans were under no obligation to save France from her folly.

Hamilton was aware that France enjoyed broad popular support in the United States, most recently demonstrated in the enthusiastic reception which the new French envoy, Genet, had received. This popular feeling raised what Hamilton treated as the sentimental objection to the proclamation, namely that it was inconsistent with gratitude for French aid during the American revolution. This sounded like an argument from morality but Hamilton treated it as an emotional response similar to an attitude of "all for love and the world well lost." Gratitude differed from justice—giving each his due—because gratitude was based on a benefit received or expected "which there is no right to claim." When benefits were bestowed for reciprocal advantages, gratitude was inoperative because payment had already been made. Thus Hamilton showed that France aided the American revolutionaries because she wanted to humble Great Britain, her great rival. Moreover, if gratitude should have any weight, Hamilton cleverly suggested, then Louis XVI, the dethroned and decapitated King of France, ought to be the beneficiary. On the whole, though, Hamilton argued that "it may be affirmed as a general principle, that the predominant motive of good offices from one nation to another is the interest or advantage of the Nation, which performs them."[44] Following Vattel, Hamilton remarked that the rule of morality in this respect was not the same between nations as between individuals. The duty of making its own welfare the guide of its actions is much stronger on the former than on the latter. (How it defines that welfare remains an important question.) In short, a policy regulated by its own advantage, as far as justice and good faith permit, is and ought to be a nation's prevailing policy.[45]

As Americanus, Hamilton considered the "cause of liberty" appeal at greater length. There were two aspects to the question as to how far regard for the cause of liberty should induce the United States to join the war on France's side: first, whether France's cause was truly the cause of liberty, "pursued with justice and humanity, and in a manner likely to crown it with honorable success." Second, what were the means available to the United States and the probable costs and benefits which would attend a policy of joining with the French? Hamilton strongly suggested that French liberty had become anarchy, and soon would become dictatorship—an astonishing prediction of Napoleon's rise.

On the second question, Hamilton concluded that the United States could do very little to help: "there is no probable prospect of this country rendering material service to the cause of France, by engaging with her in the War."[46] On the other hand, the United States would risk a great deal, perhaps its life as a nation. There were occasions, Hamilton admitted, when nations ought to hazard their existence to defend their rights and to vindicate their honor, "but let us at least have the consolation of not having rashly courted misfortune."[47]

American liberty was founded with due respect for property, personal security, and religion. In their revolution, the Americans exercised moderation and then, "without tumult or bloodshed," adopted a form of government which established "the foundations of Liberty on the basis of Justice, Order and Law."[48] All this stood in stark contrast with the licentiousness, anarchy, and atheism characteristic of French republicanism; Hamilton was anxious to make a clear distinction between the two. Practically, the "cause of liberty," which American Francophiles saw as indivisible, could be defeated in France but probably not in America. Should the Europeans defeat France and restore the monarchy, there would be all sorts of obstacles they would have to overcome to do the same in America, not the least of which would be each other. The operation of the balance of power system in Europe and the mutual jealousy of France, Spain, and Britain would assure the Americans their independence.

In 1798, however, when Hamilton discussed the probability of a French invasion of America, it was because he had concluded that the French had overthrown the European system and overcome the obstacles which existed prior to the successes of the French armies in Europe. Thus Hamilton identified the balance of power system with the European system and, just as the British identified occupation of the Low Countries with a threat to British security, so Hamilton regarded French occupation of Europe as a threat to American security. The danger of identifying French and American liberty was that such an identification might create the pretext the Europeans would otherwise lack for acting against the United States. This was all the more reason to stay out of European affairs as much as possible. Some day the United States might gain a safe preponderance of power in a global balance of power system, able, in the words of the 11th Federalist, "to dictate the terms of the connection between the old and the new world!"[49] Until then, the United States might need to form temporary alliances out of necessity and Hamilton undoubtedly saw his accommodations to British power in that light.[50]

V

The task Hamilton set for himself in defending the Jay Treaty required a much more extensive analysis, since he wanted to subject each article of the proposed agreement to review. The result was thirty-five letters entitled "The Defence" and signed "Camillus."

Because this was the defense of a treaty, Hamilton made an even greater use of rules derived from the law of nations than he had previously. In addition to arguments which he had already made about American foreign policy, Hamilton addressed the issues of impressment, free trade, contraband, and blockades, all of which warfare in Europe had forced Americans to consider as they attempted to remain neutral. Hamilton argued that the treaty conformed to the law of nations, served the interests of the United States, and did not violate the other treaties of the United States.

> [T]he Treaty lately negotiated with Great Britain does nothing but confirm by a positive agreement a rule of

the law of nations indicated by reason supported by the better opinion of writers ratified by modern usage— dictated by justice and good faith recognised by formal acts and declarations of different nations—witnessed by diplomatic testimony—sanctioned by our treaties with other countries and by treaties betweeen other countries—and conformable with sound policy and the true interest of the United States.[51]

In his defense of the Jay Treaty Hamilton argued that in the dispute with Britain over nonfulfillment of treaty obligations in the 1783 treaty there was injustice on both sides: Britain had not given up the western posts, but the United States had not secured the British debts or Loyalist property. In an analysis requested by President Washington (Hamilton had returned to private life) Hamilton wrote:

Mutual infractions of the Treaty had taken place ... it will follow that the surrender of the posts on their side would draw with it a right of compensations for the losses suffered by impediments to the recovery of the debts on our side.[52]

There was no denying British infractions of the treaty nor the additional problem of British depredations of American shipping in the war with France; the question at the time of sending Jay to England was how best to rectify the situation. Some had counseled measures to cut off commercial intercourse with Britain and sequester British debts, but the course advocated by Hamilton and taken by the Administration was "vigorous preparation for war and one more effort to avert it by negotiation."[53] He also consistently called for the nation to arm and negotiate simultaneously. If negotiations should fail, the nation would still be in a good position to press its claims through force, having armed itself in preparation for that contingency. It is wrong simply to charge Hamilton with seeking military honor at the expense of his country, because he consistently advocated negotiations as the best way for the nation to address its adversaries. Nevertheless he also concluded that at times war was indeed preferable to further negotiations, the position he reached during the administration of John Adams and the period of the quasi-war with France. This course was sanctioned by the law of nations which taught that reprisals ought to be preceded with a demand for reparations and an effort to negotiate differences between countries contemplating war; the other course was fraught with danger and injustice. To threaten war through reprisals left the other party no other choice but resort to force.

In addition, sending Jay gave the United States time to fortify its ports, supply its arsenals, raise troops, and otherwise prepare for war. This course assured all that all reasonable measures had been taken to redress injuries short of war; if war came, the country would be united. Otherwise Britain would have had the advantage of facing a divided nation. Hamilton would repeat this counsel three years later during the period of quasi-war with France when he supported sending an extraordinary mission to France because "as we sent an Envoy Extraordinary to Britain so ought we to send one to France." The underlying rule in both cases was that "we ought to do every thing to avoid rupture, without unworthy sacrifices, and to keep in view as a primary object union at home."[54]

One problem with the confrontational approach advanced by the Jeffersonians was its overestimation of American capabilities. To Hamilton it was a mistake to regard the United States "as among the first rate powers of the world," and to propose action based on that assumption. The United States simply was in no position "to give the law to Great Britain."[55] While the goals of the Jeffersonians on the free ships principle, impressment, and contraband were laudable, there were insufficient means to gain those ends. Hamilton continued to insist that peace was the real interest of the United States and ought not to be forsaken "unless the relinquishment be clearly necessary to preserve our honour on some unequivocal point, or to avoid the sacrifice of some right or interest of material and permanent importance."[56] As a general rule derived from the law of nations, it was not until after it had become manifest that reasonable reparation of a clear, premeditated wrong could not be obtained by an amicable adjustment that honor demanded a resort to arms.

Hamilton believed that Jay's mission and the Jay Treaty had achieved real gains for the United States. First and foremost, the posts were finally to be turned over to the United States. This would make it easier to address Indian problems in the west, prevent the British from trying to create an Indian buffer state between the United States and Canada, and attach the Western lands to the United States against possible Spanish or British schemes to seduce the Westerners away from the United States.[57]

In addition a spoilations commission had been established to provide for remuneration for American shipping taken by British warships. It was true that the United States made some concessions or admissions of guilt on the issue of seizure of Loyalist property, but that was the essence of the compromise which Hamilton defended: "What sensible man, what human man, will deny that a compromise which secures substantially the objects of interest is almost always preferable to war?"[58]

Vattel, in his chapter on neutrality, sanctioned the seizure of enemy property on neutral ships, provided the master of the vessel was reimbursed; he allowed the interruption of all commerce with places under seige; and he included as contraband "arms, ammunition, timber for shipbuilding, every kind of naval stores, horses, and even provisions, in certain junctures, when we have hopes of reducing the enemy by famine."[59] Hamilton admitted that the modern modifications of these harsh rules might be desirable but he did not believe that they were worth going to war to obtain. Even Jefferson, who contended for the modern neutralist definition in his letter to the French government detailing American charges against Genet, had admitted that the principle of "free ships, free goods" had not yet become a part of the established law of nations. Until Britain conceded on the point, moreover, the United States could not claim it as a right, and it would be a long time, Hamilton suspected, until the principal maritime power acceded to the new principles or until belligerent powers adhered to them in time of war.[60] Stephen Rosen has pointed out that Hamilton could make his case successfully because the law of nations was a reflection of international reality: "By demanding that American citizens obey international law, Hamilton was demanding that they obey the reality of external powers."[61] Acquiescence in the British interpretation of belligerent rights rather than insistence on the broad neutralist definition was one consequence of this view. On the other hand, without the maintenance of a balance of power system in Europe even the limited rights and choices of the weaker powers would disappear. Hamilton's acceptance of the British view on neutral rights reflected his doubt that the broad definition could ever be sustained in war and his conviction that the British were maintaining the European balance on which American security depended.

VI

If Hamilton saw his country as unable to become involved in war out of insufficient cause or weakness in 1790, 1793, or 1795, he had changed his mind by 1798. This change was prompted by (a) French attacks on American shipping, (b) continued French pretensions to universal empire, and (c) the threat of French occupation of Louisiana and invasion of the southern United States. Hamilton made these points in a series of articles written in March and April, 1798, and entitled, "The Stand." Having warned his countrymen of the danger, Hamilton characteristically called for a state of "mitigated hostility" in which the United States took measures to arm itself while at the same time pursuing one last effort to negotiate with the French. "My plan ever is to combine energy with moderation," he wrote a friend.[62]

In the naval contest with Britain, France found herself unable to act without violating neutral shipping. Indeed the principle of "free ships make free goods," which had been part of the treaty with the United States, had been laid aside as early as May 9, 1793. By 1798 the French considered every neutral ship engaged in the British carrying trade to be supportive of England and therefore an enemy to France and liable to capture. France's supporters had been embarrassed by this abandonment, though they blamed the British for making it necessary for the French to resort to those means. Because Hamilton doubted that this principle could become part of the customary law of nations, he did not dwell on these violations, except as an infringement of American rights generally. Hamilton concentrated more on the danger of France's "pretensions to universal empire," which he had warned against earlier. Many of the points he had made in Pacificus and Americanus he repeated here. France had prostrated surrounding nations, sought universal empire, decreed war against all monarchies, and invited sedition in every country, all of which were violations of the law of nations and a threat to the balance of power system. Hamilton clearly believed that the coalitions against France fought in a just cause:

> The moment the convention vomited forth those venomous decrees, all the governments were justifiable in making war. There is no rule of public law better established or on better grounds, than that whenever one nation unequivocally avows maxims of conduct danger-

ous to the security and tranquility of others, they have a right to attack her, and to endeavor to disable her from carrying her schemes into effect.[63]

Hamilton clearly sided with Britain and her claims that she acted not only in self-defense but in defense of established rights, "guaranteed by the public law of Europe, against a power for which neither established rights nor international law had any validity."[64] Britain, to be sure, had used this claim to advance her own position in international politics, but it was no less true that she had also been "an essential and an effectual shield against real danger."[65] This was a theme which Federalists like Fisher Ames would stress even more strongly than Hamilton had. In an essay entitled "The Balance of Europe," Ames maintained that

the British navy, considered in an abstract point, is too large and too superior to that of all other nations, especially our own. But naval power, it may be said, is rather less fitted for the purposes of national aggrandizement than any other. It is very likely to provoke enemies and not well adapted to subdue them. . . . If it be an evil for that navy to be so great, it is clearly a less evil than for the French power to be freed from its resistance. Remove that resistance, and France would rule the civilized world.[66]

Hamilton did more than describe French violations of the public law of Europe; he had come to the conclusion that French principles themselves must now be attacked. Where Vattel had written that religion ought not to enter into discussions of international politics, Hamilton introduced it. He had started to move in this direction in his earlier writings, but in The Stand he went much farther than he had before. To Theodore Sedgwick he wrote privately, "We must oppose to political fanaticism religious zeal."[67] He did this in two ways. First he discussed the effort among the French to destroy all religious opinion "and to pervert a whole people to atheism."[68] For Hamilton religion and morality were closely linked, and he saw in the loss of religion in France the loss of morality as well; only the terrors of despotism would be able to curb the impetuous passions of man, and to confine him within the bounds of social duty.[69] Secondly Hamilton called for a day of national fasting and prayer, which would presumably call attention to the differences between French and American liberty on the subject of religion. This new sensitivity to the political uses of religion found its ultimate conclusion in Hamilton's proposals for a "Christian Constitutional Society" which would compete with the Jeffersonian party and its "Jacobin" principles.[70]

It was only after this discussion of the French threat to the European system and to the religious dimension of civilized life that Hamilton treated French relations with the United States. Simply because France was conducting an unjust war did not mean that the United States had to enter into a coalition against her; that was clear from the distinction between the necessary and the voluntary laws of nature. However, French actions did have a direct effect on the United States which obligated the United States to act. Hamilton mentioned several concerns: French violations of American shipping, its high-handed treatment of American envoys, and its continuing aspirations in North America. The latter seemed to worry him the most. The French, by virtue of their dominance over Spain, might easily force the Spanish to cede Louisiana back to them; this effort had been widely rumored and subsequent historical research has established the French desire to regain Louisiana.[71] Conceivably even if the Spanish refused, the French might be in a position to take the territories by force, since the Spanish garrisons were known to be weak.

Hamilton seems to have considered the possibility of invasion by France very real. This was something that not even all the Federalists believed, and that the Jeffersonians ridiculed. Hamilton's case went as follows: France had real claims in North America, it had indigenous support in Louisiana, Canada, and the United States, and it had bases in the Caribbean from which a military expedition could be launched. The most substantial obstacle to such a plan, of course, would be the British navy. Evidently Hamilton thought it a real possibility that Britain could be forced to negotiate a peace treaty with France, leaving France free to conduct a campaign in North America. As another possibility, France could successfully invade Britain and seize its navy and neutralize the obstacle that way. For Hamilton, then, it was possible that the United States could be left to contend alone with the conqueror of Europe. Hamilton tried to exploit all of the wrong predictions made about the probable course of the war: the French triumphs in Europe had confounded and astonished the world and suggested that anything was possible.

While many Federalists conceded the possibility of a French invasion, they regarded it as rather remote. Washington, for example, wrote Hamilton that he was undecided about the prospects of an invasion, but he thought that Hamilton underestimated the strength of the United States.[72] This difference among the Federalists became an open rupture by the time of the 1800 elections.

Hamilton saw in the possibility of war with France an opportunity as well as a danger. In a letter to Harrison Gray Otis in early 1799, Hamilton revealed that "I have been long in the habit of considering the acquisition of those countries (Louisiana and the Floridas) as essential to the permanency of the Union, which I consider as very important to the welfare of the whole."[73] Gilbert Lycan has detailed how Hamilton attempted to prepare for the acquisition of those territories by building up military forces in the West. In the event of a war with France, which plausibly might include Spain, a military expedition under the command of General Wilkinson, in consultation with Hamilton and other government leaders, would be ready to descend the Mississippi and occupy New Orleans.[74] Little came of these plans, however. Secretary of the Treasury Oliver Wolcott doubted that the United States had the means to support a venture whose costs were unpredictable, and President John Adams was more desirous of reducing tensions with France than of possibly gaining Louisiana.

The Hamiltonian legacy, then, was one which understood the importance of the maintenance of the European balance system for the preservation of the American republic and for a law of nations which encouraged moderation. This was an important, though not the sole, reason for Hamilton's turn against France, and involved a judgment about the intentions, as well as the capabilities of both France and Great Britain. The European tradition of the law of nations and the balance of power provided criteria by which such a judgement could be made. Additionally, the Hamiltonian approach required matching foreign policy objectives with the capacity for achieving them. To speak softly because American power was far from overwhelming might have been the Hamiltonian motto. Eventually the temporary accommodations with the British would not be necessary. Finally Hamilton's approach held together two components of diplomacy which Americans since have tended to separate: to arm and to negotiate simultaneously. Americans have tended to think of war and peace as discrete conditions with no middle ground. It was the ambiguous character of international relations that concerned Hamilton. His persistent effort to anchor national policy to that reality remains his major contribution to the establishment of an American foreign policy tradition.

NOTES

1. Charles Fenwick, "The Authority of Vattel," *American Political Science Review*, VII, 3 (August 1913), p. 395.
2. Benjamin Franklin to Dumas, *The Papers of Benjamin Franklin*, ed. William Willcox (22 vols.; New Haven: Yale University Press, 1959-), XXII, 287.
3. Cited in Fenwick, "The Authority of Vattel," p. 410.
4. See for example Alexander Hamilton, "Remarks on the Treaty of Amity, Commerce, and Navigation Lately Negotiated Between the United States and Great Britain," and "The Defence," No.'s 2, 3, 6, 14, 15, 16, 18, 20, 21, 22, 31, and 32, *The Papers of Alexander Hamilton*, eds. Harold Syrett and Jacob Cooke (26 vols.; New York: Columbia University Press, 1961-1979), XVIII, 405-54, and XIX where the law of nations and Vattel figure as prominent authorities in Hamilton's argument. This source is cited hereafter as *Hamilton Papers*.
5. Hedley Bull, "The Grotian Conception of International Society," *Diplomatic Investigations*, eds. Herbert Butterfield and Martin Wight (London: Unwin and Allen, 1966), pp. 51-73. See also R. J. Vincent, *Nonintervention and International Order* (Princeton: Princeton University Press, 1974).
6. David Hume, "Of Civil Liberty," *Philosophical Works*, eds. T. H. Green and T. H. Grose (4 vols.; Darmstadt: Scientia Verlag Allen, 1964), III, 161.
7. Emmerich de Vattel, *The Law of Nations; or Principles of the Law of Nature, Applied to the Conduct and Affairs of Nations and Sovereigns*, trans. Joseph Chitty (6th ed.; Philadelphia: T. and J. W. Johnson, 1844), Preliminaries, section vii. Hereafter cited as Vattel.
8. F. S. Ruddy, *International Law in the Enlightenment* (Dobbs Ferry, N.Y.: Oceana Publications, Inc., 1975), pp. 83-84.
9. Vattel, Preliminaries, sect. lviii-lx.
10. *Ibid.*, Book I, ch. 2, sect. vii and lvi.
11. "Pacificus, No. 4," *Hamilton Papers*, XV, 86.
12. Vattel, Preliminaries, sect xvi.
13. *Ibid.*, Preliminaries, sect. xv.
14. Bull, "The Grotian Conception," pp. 54-63.
15. Vattel, Bk. III, ch. 3, sect. 47.
16. *Ibid.*
17. Edward Gulick, *Europe's Classical Balance of Power* (New York: W. W. Norton, 1955), pp. 30-33.
18. *The Records of the Federal Convention*, ed. Max Farrand (4 vols.; New Haven: Yale University Press, 1937), I, 448.
19. David Hume, "Of the Balance of Power," *Philosophical Works*, I, 350-55.

20. Charles Davenant, *Essays Upon the Balance of Power, The Right of Making War, Peace, and Alliances, and Universal Monarchy* (London: James Knapton, 1701), pp. 277-83.
21. Peter Butler, "Legitimacy in a States-System: Vattel's *Law of Nations*," *The Reason of States*, ed. Michael Donelan (London: Allen and Unwin, 1978), pp. 45-63.
22. Vattel, Bk. II, chaps. 6-7.
23. Michael Walzer, "The Moral Standing of States: A Response to Four Critics," *Philosophy and Public Affairs*, IX, 3 (Spring 1980), p. 224.
24. "The Stand, No. 2," *Hamilton Papers*, XVIII, 394.
25. Vincent, *Nonintervention and International Order*, p. 332.
26. Vattel, Bk. II, ch. 1, sect. 16.
27. *Ibid.*, Bk. II, ch. 1, sect. 4.
28. *Ibid.*, Bk. II, ch. 3, sect. 152.
29. *Ibid.*, Bk. III, ch. 3, sect. 46.
30. Alberto Coll, *Law, Theology, and History* (Washington, D.C.: University Press of America, 1982), p. 75.
31. Vattel, Bk. III, ch. 4, sect. 5
32. *Ibid.*, Bk. III, ch. 6, sect. 85.
33. For Jefferson and Madison's approach see Alfred Bowman, "Jefferson, Hamilton, and American Foreign Policy," *Political Science Quarterly*, LXXI, 1 (March 1956), pp. 18-41; Merrill Peterson, "Jefferson and Commercial Policy, 1783-1793," *William and Mary Quarterly*, 3d. series, XIV, 4 (October 1965), pp. 584-610. For a critique of this approach see Paul Varg, *Foreign Policies of the Founding Fathers* (Baltimore: Penguin Books, 1970).
34. "Nootka Sound Opinion," *Hamilton Papers*, VII, 53.
35. Alexander DeConde, *Entangling Alliance: Politics and Diplomacy Under George Washington*, (Durham, N.C.: Duke University Press, 1958), p. 5.
36. *Hamilton Papers*, VII, 52.
37. Joseph Charles, *The Origins of the American Party System*, (New York: Harper and Row, 1956).
38. "Pacificus, No. 2," *Hamilton Papers*, XV, 57.
39. *Ibid.*, p. 58.
40. To Washington, May 2, 1793, *ibid.*, XV, 407.
41. W. Allison Phillips and Arthur Reede, *Neutrality in the Napoleonic Era, Vol. II Neutrality: Its History, Economics, and Law* (New York: Columbia University Press, 1936), p. 6.
42. *Hamilton Papers*.
43. "Pacificus, No. 2," *ibid.*, XV, 59.
44. "Pacificus, No. 4," *ibid.*, p. 85.
45. *Ibid.*, p. 86.
46. "Americanus, No. 1," *ibid.*, p. 678.
47. "Americanus, No. 2," *ibid.*, XVI, 14.

48. *Ibid.*, p. 19.
49. Alexander Hamilton, John Jay, and James Madison, No. 11, *The Federalist*, ed. Clinton Rossiter (New York: New American Library, 1960), p. 91.
50. Gerald Stourzh, *Alexander Hamilton and the Idea of Republican Government* (Stanford: Stanford University Press, 1970), pp. 194-200.
51. "The Defence, No. 22," *Hamilton Papers*, XIX, 394.
52. "Remarks on the Treaty of Amity, Commerce, and Navigation," *ibid.*, XVIII, 424.
53. "The Defence, No. 2," *ibid.*, p. 493.
54. Hamilton to William L. Smith, April 5, 1797, *ibid.*, XXI, 21-22.
55. "The Defence, No. 1," *ibid.*, XVIII, 481.
56. "The Defence, No. 5," *ibid.*, XIX, 90.
57. "The Defence, No. 7," *ibid.*, pp. 115-18.
58. "The Defence, No. 3," *ibid.*, XVIII, 516.
59. Vattel, III, 7, 112-17.
60. "The Defence, No. 31," *Hamilton Papers*, XIX, p. 473-79. See also Hamilton's comments to Washington in his "Remarks on the Treaty of Amity," *ibid.*, XVIII, 437-40.
61. Stephen Rosen, "Alexander Hamilton and the Domestic Uses of International Law," *Diplomatic History*, V, 3 (Summer 1981), pp. 195-96.
62. Hamilton to William L. Smith, April 5, 1798, *Hamilton Papers*, XXI, 21.
63. "The Stand, No. 2," *ibid.*, p. 395.
64. Phillips and Reede, *Neutrality in the Napoleonic Era*, II, p. 6.
65. "The Stand, No. 4," *Hamilton Papers*, XXI, 413.
66. "Balance of Europe," *The Works of Fisher Ames*, ed. Seth Ames (2 vols.; New York: Burt Franklin, 1971), II, 234.
67. Hamilton to Sedgwick, March 15, 1798, *Hamilton Papers*, XXI, 363.
68. "The Stand, No. 3," *ibid.*, p. 402.
69. *Ibid.*, p. 405. In the Farewell Address, Washington put it this way: "Let us with caution indulge the supposition that morality can be maintained without religion. Whatever may be conceded to the influence of refined education on minds of peculiar structure, reason and experience both forbid us to expect that national morality can prevail in exclusion of religious principle." Cited in *A Compilation of the Papers and Messages of the Presidents*, ed. James Richardson (11 vols.; Washington, D.C.: Bureau of National Literature, 1911), I, 219.
70. Hamilton to James Bayard, April 16-21, 1802, *ibid.*, XXV, 605-610. See also the discussion of Douglass Adair and Marvin Harvey, "Was Alexander Hamilton A Christian Statesman?" in *Fame and the Founding Fathers*, ed. Trevor Colbourn (New York; W. W. Norton, 1974), pp. 141-59.

71. Frederick Jackson Turner, "The Origin of Genet's Projected Attack on Louisiana and the Floridas," *American Historical Review,* III, 4 (July 1897), pp. 650-71; Frederick Jackson Turner, "The Policy of France Toward the Mississippi Valley in the Period of Washington and Adams," *American Historical Review,* X, 2 (January 1905), pp. 249-279; James A. James, "French Opinion as a Factor in Preventing War Between France and the United States, 1795-1800," *American Historical Review,* XXX, 1 (October 1924), pp. 44-55. Each of these articles stresses the desire of France to regain Louisiana to check the growth of the United States, ensure American fulfillment of treaties, and acquire valuable raw materials.
72. Washington to Hamilton, May 27, 1798, *Hamilton Papers,* XXI, 470-74.
73. Hamilton to Otis, Jan. 26, 1799, *ibid.,* pp. 440-42.
74. Gilbert Lycan, *Alexander Hamilton and American Foreign Policy,* pp. 373-394. See also Hamilton's article, "For the *Evening Post*" in *Hamilton Papers,* XXVI, 82-85, where Hamilton, on hearing that Spain had ceded Louisiana back to France, recommends that the United States "seize at once on the Floridas and New Orleans, and then negotiate."

2

THOMAS JEFFERSON, REPUBLICAN VALUES, AND FOREIGN COMMERCE

Burton Spivak

During the last few years, American historians have produced an impressive amount of scholarship on the Jeffersonian era: Garry Wills and Morton White on the Declaration and the philosophy of the Revolution; Lance Banning on the Republican opposition of the 1790s; Forrest McDonald, Robert Johnstone and Noble Cunningham on Jefferson's presidency; and Drew McCoy and Ralph Lerner on the general themes of political economy and economic culture. Although these and other studies defy a simple synthesis, much of their meaning, in different ways and sometimes unintentionally, suggests an important change in our understanding of the early Republic. Thomas Jefferson, it seems, is becoming less important to what is now emerging in our literature as the central development of the post-Revolutionary years. That development no longer concerns the political order and the transition from deference to democracy, but rather the social order and the transition from "virtuous citizen" to "commercial man."[1]

As long as political freedom was the focus of history-writing, Jefferson's centrality to the early national period and his relevance to the democratizing aspects of the Age of Jackson were obvious. So too was his hold on the American imagination.[2] Washington, Hamilton, and John Adams were simply too elitist to become Democracy's symbols. Sam Adams and other authentic eighteenth-century democrats were, oddly enough, too common for democratic veneration. Jefferson survived and thrived, as John Adams knew he would, because a democratic people could find no more uncommon symbol of their political dreams. His historical importance, then, has rested on his compelling relationship to the liberal idea that government, properly constructed, is a "transaction of free men."[3] But what of *society* properly constructed? After the Revolution, what was the liberal social idea?

The modern American image of a liberal society began to emerge with some clarity in the Age of Jackson. By then its ideal had become the legitimate power of self-interest, washing through unobstructed markets of free entrepreneurs, hedged in only by public opinion and voluntary contract enforceable at law.[4] In the generation before the Civil War this market metaphor attached itself to many kinds of human production and social activity. Everything from political creeds to religious beliefs, from land and money to medicine and literature, became vendible commodities in an overlapping series of open markets. Society, in short, was becoming a marketplace. And active competition in the free market, so the ideal held, would promote excellence, insure mobility and status, and even create values. It was the market, not elite groups and national institutions, that would both release private energy and sort the claims of contentious individuals on behalf of the public good.

By the mid-nineteenth century, the social counterpart of a free politics of independent men was becoming a competitive society of enterprising agents. For mid-century democrats, self-interest had become a positive attribute and the foundation of a just social order. This revolution in values, so pronounced by the Civil War, began less confidently with the Jeffersonians' attempt to square their classical republican beliefs with the economic opportunities of the post-Revolutionary commercial world. Ironically, Jefferson always felt at odds with this crucial accommodation. Granted that on the plane of politics, Jefferson is an important link between the dreams of the Revolution and the fulfillment of the Jacksonians. But because he did not understand society as a marketplace, because he rejected Destutt de Tracy's notion that "justice is founded in contract solely,"[5] Jefferson was not really involved in the supreme intellectual effort to create the outlines of a new social order that could safely house the competitive commercial energies of what Ralph Lerner has called the "Anglo-American New-Model Man."[6]

Many of Jefferson's policies, from his opposition to banks,

public debt, and paper money, to his territorial ambitions for the young republic that culminated in the Louisiana Purchase, were in some fashion connected to his strong misgivings about commerce and the kind of society it symbolized. So too was his hostility—long enduring and genuine—to the Federalist Party and its patron: Great Britain. "The English had been a wise, a virtuous, and a truly estimable people," Jefferson observed in 1813. "But commerce and a corrupt government have rotted them to the core." It was precisely because Jefferson found "commercial avarice" incompatible with "the principles of free government," that he became the enemy of England, and of English ways in America. As much as its maritime power, Jefferson feared "English books, English prejudices, and English manners," and their pernicious impact on American development.[7] To protect the republic from such evils fixed Jefferson's foreign and domestic priorities into a reasonably coherent design, just as this goal made his thinking somewhat irrelevant to the beginnings of a modern social order in America.

II

To call Jefferson anticommercial seems to run counter to the objective facts of his public life. Through much of it, it seems, this Virginia agrarian looked to the sea. One of the consistent threads in his diplomacy was the idea of free commercial access to foreign markets. His first state paper, *A Summary View of the Rights of British North America,* written in 1774, cast the Anglo-American disagreement squarely in commercial terms and outlined the commercial goals that would challenge Jefferson through most of his career. The *Summary View* pointed repeatedly to arbitrary English violations of America's "natural right [to] a free trade with all parts of the world." When it listed "the great principles of right and wrong" dividing England from America, commercial oppression preceded unfair taxation. When it outlined the only acceptable foundation of a continuing Anglo-American connection, its language and substance were explicitly commercial. Prior to the cataclysm of 1776, Jefferson still believed that trade with the English should form an important element of America's economic life, where appropriate and mutually beneficial. "But let them not think to exclude us from going to other markets," he warned.[8] That commerce should be free had become a Revolutionary article of faith. Both Jefferson's Declaration and the Congress's Model Treaty of 1776 amplified the creed, as Adam Smith's famous book provided its intellectual foundation.

Jefferson spent a long life in the service of this creed. He traveled to Europe in the 1780s to help liberate the world market on the principle of free trade. His years in Washington's cabinet turned on the two goals of expanding commerce and aligning the republic on the side of European liberty, both without involving the young nation in war.[9] During his presidency, he used diplomacy, economic weapons, and military threats to promote trade in the Mediterranean, and on the Mississippi and the Atlantic. Throughout it all, however, Jefferson's encounter with commerce was laced with doubts and second thoughts. Foreign trade was both necessary and dangerous, a vital part of his republican dream and yet its potential undoing. In many ways, Jefferson's public life hinged on this complex and ambivalent commercial vision.

Most important in justifying commerce was the simple fact that the underdeveloped state of the domestic economy required foreign markets for American agriculture. While this dependency was threatening, it was not unwelcome; in fact it was of the utmost importance to the Republican scheme of social and political development. In a transaction that lay at the heart of the Republican economic persuasion, the Jeffersonians were willing to risk *national* dependency on foreign markets to prevent the growth of *personal* dependency in America, and with it the inevitable decay of representative government. It seemed that only by leaving its workshops and customers in Europe could the United States avoid the adverse social and political consequences of large-scale industrialism. Industry on the English model presumed pools of dependent people, a social demography ill-suited to a free politics. As grim as this industrial image was, the Jeffersonians were equally apprehensive about its opposite: a primitive agricultural subsistence. The only alternative seemed to be a prosperous, worldwide commercial exchange of raw materials for finished goods. Foreign trade was thus an important component of the Republican social and political design.[10]

As important as commerce was, however, it still posed fundamental problems, which existed in two overlapping contexts: commerce as *national activity,* and commerce as *individual vocation.* With regard to the first, Jefferson feared that commerce usually bred international conflict and war. He saw the source of this tendency in European mercantilism. That reactionary ideology had transformed trade into a national weapon and tied its course to the power and interests of the political state. In the process it

32

sacrificed individual economic rights and clogged the world's ports with myriad restrictions. These political devices inhibited the natural exchange of productivity and fueled the national hatreds for the wars that usually followed. It seemed illogical to Jefferson that whereas production was a private, individual act, the right to exchange—an absolutely essential aspect of the productive right—had been appropriated by the state. Without the right to exchange, the right to produce had little real value. To return this right of exchange to the private citizen was the American Revolution's most liberal economic idea.

John Adams and Benjamin Franklin had already begun this effort when Jefferson joined them in Europe in 1784. Because reason was on the side of right, he began his diplomacy with typical optimism. Throughout the American leg of his journey—from Virginia to Boston where he intended to sail to France—he recorded in happy detail the particular American products that would find ready sale in European markets once trade had been placed on a free and natural footing.[11] Armed with little more than their free trade notions—our "liberal sentiments," John Adams called them—the American diplomats tried to transform Europe.[12] Their outline of a sensible world economy rested on a complete division between the political state and economic man. They hoped to emancipate trade from national rivalry through the medium of negotiated treaties that would finally erase national distinctions in the world market. Natives and aliens would enjoy similar rights in all commercial ports. Revolutionary diplomacy aimed at nothing less that the peaceful and complete liberation of international commercial activity implied in the term "world citizen." It was an incredibly naive undertaking and it largely failed, even when the goal became the less lofty one of "most favored nation" reciprocity.

This failure to fashion a world economy drained of political power and geared to private transactions forced the Revolutionary generation to embrace its own brand of mercantilism geared to the retaliatory power of a congressionally harnessed American market. Unable to depoliticize the world market, the United States had no choice but to politicize its own. American diplomats learned this first. "If we cannot obtain reciprocal Liberality," John Adams warned from London, "we must adopt reciprocal Prohibitions. . . . We must not be the Bubbles of our own Liberal Sentiments. We must not be the Dupes."[13] Jefferson echoed these thoughts from Paris. Because Europe would not even consider free trade, he confessed, "we shall be obliged to adopt a system which may shackle them in our ports, as they do us in theirs."[14] But to play this European game required greater amounts of domestic political consolidation than had been deemed either necessary or safe only a few years before; consequently, the liberal odyssey begun by Adams and Jefferson in Europe was concluded on a more conservative note by Madison and Hamilton in Philadelphia in 1787. In the process, the leaders of the early Republic, especially those who would become the leaders of the Republican Party in the 1790s, had found their national commercial weapon: a politicized American market.

After the Constitutional settlement of 1787, a new stage began in America's economic relationship with the Old World, because its national government could finally withhold the privilege of the American market in rhythm with foreign mistreatment of American export trade. The restriction of foreign imports was the essence of Jefferson's policy of peaceable economic coercion, a policy which in theory never included an economically destructive and politically divisive embargo on American shipping and exports. The strategies of embargo and economic coercion were separate aspects of Jeffersonian statecraft, each with its own purpose and rationale. An embargo was a defensive, precautionary tactic that temporarily withheld ships and property from the world's oceans because war was considered imminent or probable. Economic coercion, on the other hand, was a mercantilist tool of commercial diplomacy that threatened or actually restricted foreign access to the American market. Although part of its rationale was an antagonistic world economy of national rivalries, another part was the hope that economic weapons could protect American trade without war.[15]

But could economic coercion protect trade and preserve peace? That was both the dream and the doubt, and a large part of Jefferson's anxiety about commerce. Champion as Jefferson did the weapon's utility, misgivings often crowded in. In a brooding perspectus written while he was still in Europe, Jefferson acknowledged that "our commerce on the ocean and in other countries must be paid for by frequent war. The justest dispositions possible in ourselves, will not secure us against it."[16]

Although this persistent gap between trade and peace dampened Jefferson's enthusiasm for commerce, there were other doubts that were more disturbing than the war-related ones, because they could not be addressed even by separating world commerce from the web of national rivalry, or by tailoring that perfect instrument of peaceable coercion. These other doubts were more intractable because they concerned private commercial behavior itself rather than foreign restrictions on national commercial freedom. When the focus switched from the commercial needs of the American republic to the commercial life of the republican citizen, Jefferson confronted dangers that hinged on the implications of the commercial vocation for the qualities of individual character on which he thought the republican political experiment rested.

For Jefferson, the crux of a republican political order was majority rule through popular institutions composed of representatives of the people's choosing. In the early going of the Revolution, he spoke confidently about this bright possibility, about the innate popular capacity for self-government; about how the American people had exchanged the monarchical form for the republican seemingly without effort: "with as much ease," he noted, "as would have attended their throwing off an old, and putting on a new suit of clothes."[17] The casualness of Jefferson's metaphor obscured the complex transition then taking place in American politics. In addition, on this occasion and many others, Jefferson combined his sunny language about American freedom, French freedom, indeed about the universal implications of 1776, with his genuine belief that God had intended man for society and self-government. Could the contrary of this be proved, he once ventured, "I should conclude either that there is no God, or that he is a malevolent being." All of this supports the notion that Jefferson was freedom's ideologue while John Adams, more sober and historical, was its more critical servant.[18]

Although Jefferson was less tentative than Adams about man's capacity for political freedom, he was as careful a student of its necessary environment. Balanced against his liberal faith in man's moral capacity for self-government was a conservative emphasis on the fragility of this capacity and on the proper social soil necessary for its development.[19] This moral capacity, or virtue, was freighted with ambiguous meaning in the eighteenth century, but all the ambiguities turned on the general theme of sacrifice. Virtue connoted the benevolent capacity to deny or transcend self, and was thus an ironic key to the republican dream of individual freedom.

Franklin's understanding of virtue was the most modern because his stress on frugality, thrift, and personal industry made the subject and the object of the sacrificial act synonymous; the autonomous individual merely sacrificed present for future self by deferring immediate gratification for greater long-range rewards.

Although Adams and Jefferson both rejected this privatization of virtue, they differed sharply on the precise object of the benevolent act. For the New Englander, the object of benevolence was always vague, distant, and corporate; in other words, the state or the public good. For the Virginian, however, the object of virtuous behavior was much less abstract, located instead in the immediate circle of human relationships. "The essence of virtue," he wrote on countless occasions, "is in doing good to others." In this scheme, man's capacity for disinterest and sympathetic behavior became the foundations of both private morality and political liberty in America. Responsible freedom, "both public and private," was located "in a good heart," put there by "creation" so "that no error of reasoning or speculation might lead us astray."[20] Because of the importance of personal virtue to a republican politics, and because of the nurturing or corrupting impact of social milieu on it, Jefferson's political creed required a particular social foundation. In this regard he paid close attention to vocation in America, returning to it often as a determinant of private character and therefore of the public order as well.

Jefferson's anticommercialism, then, was at its core political. "Merchants love nobody," he once wrote. They act according to the "dictate [of] interest" without "love or hatred to anybody."[21] The commercial vocation bred manipulative skills, entrepreneurial abilities, a strategic mentality, and a cold heart. Agriculture was also a vocation concerned with profit. But it was "wholesome labor" that earned "honest reward." It also surrounded the individual with nature's rhythms, and "family associations [and] a society of real friends," which softened competitive urges, and fostered cooperative ones.[22] In short, Jefferson's political science connected occupation to character, and both of these to political freedom. "It is my principle," he wrote Madison, "that the will of the majority should prevail. This reliance cannot deceive us, as long as we remain virtuous; and I think we shall be so, as long as agriculture is our principal object." "Indeed, it seems to me," he wrote on another occasion, "that in proportion as commercial avarice advances on us from north and east, the principles of free government are to retire to the agricultural states. . . . With honesty and self-government for her portion, agriculture may abandon . . . to others the fruits of commerce."[23]

Because Jefferson did not understand majority rule as the political resolution of economic conflicts predicated on self-interest, he saw in the spread of self-interest, the salient aspect of the commercial vocation, the undoing of republican government in America. Commerce and its mentality, like slavery and its corruptions and paper money and its evils, was a snake in the republican garden. A commercial society of self-interested entrepreneurs would inevitably create a politics of self-interest, a republican anomaly. But some commerce was necessary to avoid both agricultural stagnation and industrialism, with its crowded cities and dependent people. Commerce as national activity, commerce as individual vocation was a central theme of Jefferson's public life: the attempt to make commerce compatible with republicanism.

III

To manage the nation's commerce in republican fashion required, above all, that it be as closely connected to agriculture as possible. "We have no occasion for more commerce than to take off our superfluous produce," he asserted in 1787. "A steady application to agriculture with just trade enough to take off its superfluities is our wisest course."[24] This kind of trade promoted agricultural development and seemed not to require massive naval and military support, which were anathema to republican principles. In the event of European war, it was less likely than the carrying trade to provoke belligerent reprisals. Although doubts lingered, a commerce in American goods on American ships seemed potentially compatible with economic prosperity, and the dreams of peace, limited government, and a republican social and political order. All these things—and especially a republican society of honest relationships and moral sense, and a republican politics of representative institutions composed of virtuous men—comprised the Jeffersonian national interest. It had one other essential attribute: it was anti-English.[25]

"A proud, hectoring, carnivorous race," Jefferson called the English. He wished, he told John Adams, that there was "an ocean of fire between that Island and us."[26] What are we to make of such sentiments and language, especially since anti-English statements were so common to Republican political rhetoric? How are we to separate conventional thoughts ritualized into trite language and political slogans from the genuine passionate article?

Even a casual reading of the writings of the leading Republicans shows that Jefferson's anglophobia was deeper, more persistent, and more central to his whole orientation than the usual garden variety. There was a personal dimension to his anglophobia, a relationship to his maturing identity and his capacity for Revolutionary activity that invites the methods of the careful psychohistorian. Jefferson's whole life seemed to bear witness to the pain of separation and the desire to keep family, friends, and relationships together. In the years preceding Revolution, Jefferson was a philosophical patriot but a psychological Tory. To embrace Revolution, Jefferson first had to clear a psychological path toward separation by magnifying both America's innocence and England's willful betrayal of familial trust. Jefferson's language indicates that the final separation had a personal dimension for him. He wrote of the Anglo-American break that "there can be no medium between those who have loved so much." The Congress deleted from his Declaration the phrase about "the last stab to agonizing affection."[27] Jefferson's intense and sometimes morbid anglophobia was the permanent emotional cost of his capacity for Revolutionary activity, and a continuing source of his Republican identity. He often defined the Republic itself through negative references to Great Britain. English society had been thoroughly corrupted by self-interest and commercialism. It nurtured either condescension and dependence, or manipulative relationships. He thought diplomacy with the English futile because "an American contending by strategem against those exercised in it from their cradle would undoubtedly be outwitted by them."[28] Indeed, he saw in the Hamiltonian political and economic systems a betrayal of republican dreams and a dangerous duplication of an English model of government and society, a society comprised of countinghouses and workhouses wherein a commercial and industrial class, debased by luxury, lived off the labor of the numerous poor, who were debased by tedium and want.[29]

For all these reasons, Jefferson was leery of closer commercial relations with England, even if they could be achieved on advantageous terms. And this he never believed could happen, so wedded was England to commercial monopoly, its "national disease," its "insanity," as Jefferson called it.[30] To divert trade from England and toward the Continent became a central goal of his diplomacy. Although Jefferson often spoke about economic retaliation against England, it was rarely to improve Anglo-American trade *per se*, but rather to clear the English out of the Northwest; to open up their Caribbean Islands (the only trade with them he ever coveted); to improve America's standing with other European courts; or to coerce England's acceptance of America's neutral right to trade with England's enemies.[31]

So a foreign trade tilted away from England and toward the Continent, a peacetime trade in American goods on American ships, this was for Jefferson the sum of the nation's commercial interest. But when he became president, England still monopolized the American trade, and for unavoidable reasons: the availability of English credit, the absence of other viable trading partners, and the American preference for English goods. Jefferson himself once refused to buy a French harness, even though his comrade Lafayette made the purchase a point of republican honor, because the English variety was more to his taste: "It is not from a love of the English but a love of myself," he confessed, "that I sometimes find myself obliged to buy their manufactures." Jefferson's own inclination, multiplied thousands-fold throughout American society, created an English pattern to American trade that was as persistent as it was troubling.[32]

Whether the markets were English, Continental, or Caribbean, the essential point remains that only a peacetime trade in American goods conformed to Republican economic philosophy. However, the goals of Jefferson's presidential diplomacy had a much different commercial emphasis, and by his own reckoning, a more dangerous and less republican one. In fact, the economic goals of Jefferson's English diplomacy became little more than the assertion of a national right to the lucrative wartime carrying trade in the goods of England's enemies and their colonial possessions. This imperial trade was generally off-limits to American ships during peacetime. But when pressed by war and the Royal Navy, England's enemies gladly opened this trade to neutral carriers. So it was that during the Napoleonic War, the United States tried to assume the role of prosperous middleman, transporting French and Spanish goods between colonies and mother countries.

The Jeffersonians were men of peace who calculated the benefits of European war too heavily into their accounting of American prosperity. Although Republican economic theory pegged agricultural prosperity to the legitimate penetration of foreign markets for native products during peacetime, Republican leaders claimed as a national right a foreign commerce tied to European war. In short, the Jeffersonians enlisted international law on behalf of national avarice. "Neutrals have at all times been avaricious and encroachers," Benjamin Stoddert would write Jefferson in 1809. "Had we been ever so certain that the belligerent nations would have submitted to [our] encroachments . . . , we should still have decided from regard to our own interest that none should have

39

been made—and we should have still confined our enterprise to a commerce purely American."[33] The Republicans, when in power, might have better managed the nation's affairs had they followed their own distinction between natural and artificial economic development. To the extent that they denied their own best instincts and embraced the Anglo-French war as a profitable enterprise, they contributed to the problems that confounded Jefferson's presidency and produced an unnecessary war during that of his successor.

IV

The Jeffersonian defense of the wartime carrying trade is a particularly revealing window on a pattern common to much subsequent American diplomatic experience. The initial defense never had Jefferson's wholehearted support. The carrying trade became an administrative measure merely because not to defend it created significant political risks at home, and to defend it successfully seemed only to require a strong legal and moral argument on its behalf. The defense became costly only after England, the nation that stood to lose the most from America's claim, refused to accept the logic of Jefferson's explanation of "honest neutrality," and backed this refusal with force. The English challenge provoked Jefferson's nationalism and anglophobia, and thereby deepened a policy commitment that his republicanism had found objectionable. The climax to this conflict of nationalistic anger and republican guilt occurred when Jefferson, in the midst of the embargo crisis, renounced foreign trade completely and fashioned a new political economy that transformed his agrarianism and significantly altered his attitude toward the relationship between the Old World and the New. The denouement, sketched in letters when Jefferson was out of power, maintained this new orientation with only slight modification.

Whether the carrying trade was a prudent national objective attainable without excessive cost or war, indeed whether it was a worthy republican objective at all, were questions that had troubled Jefferson since the beginnings of the disintegration of European peace in the 1780s. The trade fed on war and was therefore unseemly. It upset the republican design by divorcing trade from agriculture. Because it also divorced productivity from profit, it promoted "commercial avarice," "speculation," and "a spirit of gambling," all unrepublican vices. And because it would become little more than a French trade covered by an American flag, it was in fact not neutral, and would certainly provoke a stern response from Great Britain. For all these reasons, Jefferson never really departed from his candid 1780s assessment of the carrying trade: "At first blush a war [between England and France] would promise advantage to us. . . . Yet I think we shall lose in happiness and morals by being launched again into the ocean of speculation, led to overtrade ourselves, [and] tempted to become sea-robbers under French colours."[34]

Both economic and political pressures weakened Jefferson's commitment to a prudent and republican commercial policy and "launched" his administration onto "an ocean of speculation" and troubles. The carrying trade was very profitable. There was also the political need of the Republican Party in New England. Jefferson's nationalism invariably surfaced whenever England pinched, regardless of the propriety of American demands, and Jefferson's exquisite rationalism often equated tight argument with sound policy. "I send you a pamphlet," Jefferson wrote a friend in 1806, "in which the British doctrine that a commerce not open to neutrals in peace shall not be pursued by them in war is logically and unanswerably refuted."[35] Language was Jefferson's medium — language, logic, and persuasion. A good case could exorcise doubts and enable policy to take care of itself. A perfect case would give the rational world no choice but to nod its assent. Jefferson went to great lengths to prove the fairness and legality of American demands, as much to himself as anyone else. Great Britain, so his argument ran, benefited more from the American market than did France. This advantage canceled whatever benefit France might derive from America's neutral carriage. "We shall thus become what we sincerely wish to be," he wrote, "honestly neutral and truly useful to both belligerents: to the one by keeping open a market for the consumption of her manufactures; to the other by securing for her a safe carriage of all her productions, metropolitan or colonial, while [her] own means are restrained by [her] enemy."[36] Words had transformed the nation's role on the high seas. No longer a grasping neutral, Jefferson's America had become a benevolent servant to a war-torn world. The argument may have quieted Republican guilt, but it neither convinced England nor handled the needs of policy.

England responded in 1805 with the *Essex* ruling that overturned the *Polly* decision of 1800.[37] In the *Polly* case, English courts gave the United States restricted but profitable access to the carrying trade by removing it from the constraints of the Rule of 1756.

(That Rule denied to neutrals any trade that England's enemies did not grant them in peacetime.) *Polly* allowed the carrying trade if the voyage was interrupted (broken) by an importation into the neutral country. Under *Polly,* an American shipper could carry colonial cargoes to Europe if he first stopped in an American port, unloaded, paid duties, and then reloaded, preferably on another ship. According to *Polly,* the Rule of 1756 did not apply in such cases because all these steps changed the nationality of the cargo from belligerent to American. However, such cargoes were still subject to English rulings on contraband and blockade.

Yankee ingenuity soon reduced these cumbersome steps to a ritual. Often merchants did not even pay duties, but only posted bond. A Congressional statute allowed the American merchant to "draw back" any duties he actually paid. In practice, cargoes went unloaded, and ships unchanged. When England complained, the State Department answered that America's internal commercial arrangements were not England's concern. England's answer was the ruling in the *Essex* case that the cargo's final destination determined its nationality and whether the Rule of 1756 applied. If the cargo wound up in a Spanish port, for example, it was Spanish, carried there illegally by an American vessel even if there had been an intermediate import into an American port, and even if the duties had been paid. This ruling, if vigorously applied, threatened the American carrying trade with wholesale captures and condemnations.

Jefferson's response to the dangerous maritime environment which the *Essex* ruling created was ambivalent. There were only two options available to the United States. It could accept England's judicial innovation and navigate on a more dangerous, but still profitable, ocean as best it could. Or it could try to change that environment with diplomacy or power. Jefferson adopted the second course, but only halfheartedly. The carrying trade had his support at the beginning of his second term, but only if pamphlets and persuasion could protect it. His doubts on the propriety of the whole business left him lukewarm to stronger measures then being touted by its Northern advocates in Congress. Jefferson's pronouncements bounced between national assertion and republican restraint, but his policy, unable to relate the two in coherent fashion, simply drifted. His uncertainty on the direction of policy left its formulation to the Republican congressional majority.

The 1806 congressional response to England's commercial challenge turned on regional economic interest. The crux of the matter was that while the *Essex* decision threatened the North's wartime carrying trade, it posed little threat to the South's direct commodity trade with its best customer, Great Britain. Congressmen from carrying trade states wanted to shut the American market to all English imports, the classic Republican economic weapon. This goal eluded them because Southern Republicans opposed a policy that would dry up government revenues, postpone the retirement of the national debt, menace the South's agriculture, and risk war. These unwelcome facts seemed undeniable. "The proper arguments" for those who thought otherwise, John Randolph implored, "were a straight waistcoat, a dark room, water gruel, and depletion."[38] Contained in the Southern Republicans' opposition to British exclusion was a precise formulation of the national interest that stressed debt retirement, agriculture, and what they called "honest" or "useful trade." Wartime carriage, on the other hand, was "a mushroom," a "fungus." Its pursuit also raised disturbing questions about the moral content of the national interest, questions about whether, in John Taylor's words, "the Lord of hosts" or "the God of peace" should inspire American economic development. "Take care of the Commonwealth," he warned James Madison. "It has deeper interest than the carrying trade."[39] To protect this kind of trade with words was one thing; but to use stronger weapons, either economic or military, required the public marriage of republicanism to foreign war. At this misalliance Southern congressional Republicans balked.

Instead they helped pass a watered-down nonimportation law, with its implementation date postponed almost a year. An intellectual fascination with the power of the American market as a coercive weapon was an important component of Republican statecraft, intruding and demanding a hearing whenever the need for policy arose. But during Jefferson's presidency, theory and policy never converged for the Republicans.[40] The stakes were too narrow in 1806. The result was, in John Randolph's words, "a dose of chicken broth to be taken nine months hence."[41] The English military attack on the *Chesapeake* in the summer of 1807 so outraged Jefferson that he favored war, not the peaceable alternative of economic coercion. And although Jefferson's famous embargo of December, 1807, would eventually be pressed into service as an economic weapon of coercion, it had far different origins.

V

Like most significant commitments of national purpose, the embargo began innocently enough; it was not really a policy at all as Jefferson conceived it, but more an attempt to buy time, "an intervening period" he called it, an expedient, a temporary bow to the realities of European power and to the deterioration of America's commercial position in a volatile world. The threats had multiplied. To its attacks on the carrying trade, England, through various Orders in Council, now added restrictions on the wartime pattern of American trade in its own goods. Napoleon matched these commercial restrictions to the extent of his ability with his Berlin and Milan decrees. France's behavior finally drew Jefferson's attention to the European dimension of America's problem. Trade anywhere seemed likely to ignite war while America was grossly unprepared, with much of its maritime wealth still at sea. Jefferson's embargo aimed at little more than keeping American ships and sailors—the nation really—out of "harm's way."[42] The difficult decisions about the embargo's relationship to policy still awaited the Jeffersonians in the wake of Europe's refusal to accept a definition of neutral rights that they were unwilling to abandon.

As elusive as the embargo's policy ends were, they still did not include economic coercion. Most Jeffersonians understood that an embargo was simply the wrong economic weapon. It would hurt America more than it hurt Europe. It would strangle foreign trade in order to protect it. It would punish exports, not imports. The embargo was not the embodiment of Republican statecraft, but its caricature. In the embargo's early going, the Jeffersonians understood these stern facts and shaped policy within them. They understood that domestic economic desires would soon rob the embargo of time. Simply put, the American people would not tolerate a long-term embargo; and a short-term embargo, as a coercive weapon, was a contradiction in terms.[43]

How could the administration find coercive power in a policy that the American people would soon force it to abandon? By the spring of 1808 the Jeffersonians had found an answer, and only then did the embargo become a realistic weapon in their hands. But its utility came to rest not on the economic pain that its indeterminate continuation might inflict on Europe, but on the economic pain it was inflicting every day on the American people. Soon they would demand the repeal of the embargo, no later than at year's end. And repeal, if the European commercial restrictions still remained in force, would lead directly to war. This was the message that the administration instructed its diplomats (William Pinkney in London and John Armstrong in Paris) to convey to the belligerents. Whatever coercive power the embargo possessed—a coercive power measured only by its ability to change European policy—derived not from America's lengthy withdrawal from the world market, but rather from the threat of war with America that was implicit in the embargo's necessarily short-lived duration.[44]

By mid-1808, it was Jefferson's fondest hope that the United States could once more turn the European balance to its advantage. The gist of the diplomacy was this: each ambassador was to tell his respective government that the embargo would be taken off American trade not later than December, 1808, the beginning of the next Congressional session. When the embargo was lifted, the United States would simultaneously resume trade with whichever belligerent had removed its restrictions and declare war against whichever belligerent kept its commercial restrictions in force. If both belligerents obliged, the United States could have its trade and be spared a war. If neither belligerent did, the United States would, in Jefferson's phrase, "take our choice of enemies between them." War against both was never contemplated. But delcaring war against England—still the Republicans' chief enemy—while the French decrees still operated would create serious political divisions at home. So the Republicans hedged their bets with a strategy to insure a manageable war against a single enemy, without foreclosing the grander diplomatic objective of trade and peace. With incredible naivete, they thought they could tilt their offers dramatically in France's favor without killing the possibility of accord with Great Britain as well.[45]

The bias in the two ostensibly equal offers was contained in the fiction that there was a legal difference between ocean-based and land-based belligerent commercial restrictions. The administration insisted that only maritime restrictions violated international law and neutral rights. These restrictions were only marginally important to the French war effort, although they underwrote England's. Land-based or port restrictions, on the other hand, were France's strength, and they afflicted England and the United States with equal fury. But because of the need for a manageable war these restrictions became, in Jefferson's phrase, "vigorously legal, tho' not friendly."[46] The bias toward France seemed to insure Minister Armstrong's success in Paris. Madison told him to emphasize that what the United States was in fact demanding of France "would . . . immaterially diminish its operations against the British, that operation being so completely in the power of France on land, and so little in her power on the high seas."[47] Armstrong's trump, however, was Pinkney's embarassment in London. It offended his intelligence, he so much as told his secretary of state, to have to peddle to England so transparently a pro-French policy. In the end, both France and England rejected the American offers. Madison could not believe it. "It would seem," he wrote Armstrong in anger, "as if the [French] imperial cabinet had never paid sufficient attention to the smallness of the sacrifice" that the United States had required.[48]

Would the administration have gone to war against England if France had obliged. This is a proper inference from Jefferson's diplomacy, but a doubtful inference from the essential character of the Jeffersonians. The policies of 1808 that connected the embargo's coercive power to the promise of war had about them a false bravado, almost like children whistling past the graveyard. When the bogeyman appeared, the bravado vanished, and the administration could not, as Jefferson had promised in March, "take our choice of enemies between them." The Republicans were consequently left with an embargo they did not want, because its alternative was the war that they finally could not accept.

Beyond this, the 1808 scenario underscores the bright rationality that often blinded the Jeffersonians. Caught up in the seductive logic of their own policies, they never considered that their reasoning might appear illogical or naive from a different point of view—say from that of another nation. They became trapped in their fictions, so trapped that they were ill-prepared for failure and the hard choices they would then inherit. As a result, the embargo became the weapon of economic coercion that Jefferson never intended it to be, but only because the alternatives appeared worse. It was out of desperation at the end of his presidency that Jefferson, in the words of a Massachusetts Republican, felt impelled "to hug the embargo and die in its embrace."[49]

In this way, an economically coercive embargo became the Republicans' final defense of neutral rights and the nation's wartime commerce. But it became much more. Frustrations long pent up and doubts and anxieties long obscured welled over the surface and transformed this ill-starred policy one last time. During its last few months, Jefferson renounced not only a commerce tied to European war but, more audaciously, an economy tied to foreign trade itself. A lifetime in the service of commerce had ended in disaster. Never again, if the embargo could make it so, would the republic pay such a heavy price for merchant avarice. The embargo would redeem agricultural America, even if it had to transform the meaning of agrarianism to include urban workers. From the pain of the embargo would emerge a fully republican economy, internally diverse, independent of foreign markets, honestly productive in its rural and urban dimensions, and weaned from "the jealousy among our commercial men" that had visited such trauma on the nation.

The embargo became the nation's renewal and Jefferson's contrition. Throughout his presidency he had supported, against his own instincts, all the demands of Northern commerce. Indeed, said one sympathetic New Englander, the Jeffersonians "are friendly to commerce *overmuch*. They waste themselves in defending it in all the immunities that its self-styled friends *claim* for it." Jefferson now cursed the same trade that his diplomacy had struggled to defend. "This exuberant commerce," he wrote in anger toward the end of his term, "is now bringing war on us." When he renounced foreign trade and found sanctuary in a new republican economy that existed largely in his imagination and would take decades to implement in society, his own involvement in the nation's quest of wartime profit fueled the rejection, shaped the new dream, and gave the embargo its most poignant relevance.[50]

The emotions and hatreds—against Europe and commerce—that had surfaced with such fury during the embargo spent themselves during the long years of Jefferson's retirement. Hatred of the Old World gave way to an inevitable sense of proper distance. He now spoke as calmly about the validity of the idea of "two hemispheres" as he had once spoken euphorically about the possibilities of European redemption implied in the American Revolution. No longer an augury of European rebirth, Jefferson's republic had become, instead, "a splendid libel" on the Old World. In these calmer emotions lay the origins of the Monroe Doctrine, just as his dream of a fully independent economy anticipated Henry Clay's American System.[51] This economic dream underwent modification when the passions of his presidency abated, and there was now room in it for some foreign commerce, but only a fully republican commerce. Writing to John Adams in 1815, Jefferson asked: "Have our commercial citizens merited from their country its encountering another war to protect their gambling enterprises? The transportation of our own produce in our own vessels . . . I hold to be fundamental. . . . But whether we shall protect the mere agency of our merchants and shipowners in carrying on the commerce of other nations," he hoped, such claims would never find their way again into American commercial policy.[52] The circle was completed. Jefferson the Sage lived long enough to repudiate the policies of Jefferson the President.

VI

It is risky to generalize about the conduct of American foreign policy since the Revolution because the United States had changed so dramatically in its relatively short history. By most objective standards, the United States was an unimportant country in the Age of Jefferson. A nation of several million people living on the periphery of world power and influence, it had almost no army and a tiny navy. Its backward economy had no industry to speak of, and its agricultural regions were heavily dependent on foreign markets. Its political system was so fragmented and decentralized that much of Europe thought it would break apart at the first true national crisis (which is precisely what happened in the American Civil War). By contrast, since 1945 the United States, by any measure of power and influence, has been at the center of world affairs.

These contrasting situations created unique foreign policy challenges for different leadership groups separated by time and circumstance. Nonetheless, the twentieth-century version of America— industrial, democratic, imperial—has encountered and interacted with the external world in roughly the same fashion as did its early nineteenth-century agrarian counterpart. There has been a consistent style to American diplomacy because foreign policies are partly shaped by national self-images—and these American images have had little to do with the objective facts of American history. Although the United States was once an underdeveloped and weak nation, Americans of the eighteenth century never thought of their country as anything less than the most important place in the world. Well before the United States had global might, it had global purpose. From the beginning, the United States imagined itself a providential country, a nation that would redeem history because it transcended history.

This sense was both religious and secular; in fact, the dominant expressions of early American identity—puritanism and republicanism—were related aspects of American exceptionalism.[53] In short, American identity preceded the American experience; it was not fashioned and refashioned by it. Objectively, America is a story of change. Subjectively, the story continues where it began: from John Winthrop's "City on a hill," to Thomas Jefferson's "empire of liberty," to Abraham Lincoln's "last, best hope of mankind," to John Kennedy's claim of responsibility for free peoples everywhere.

This sense of ideological importance and global significance did not, in the early going, require an assertive, interventionist foreign policy beyond the rim of continental America.[54] So confident was the nineteenth-century republic that it was on the cutting edge of history, so sure was it that the future development of the world would duplicate in all essentials what had transpired in 1776, that the United States, in order to witness the world transformed, had only to survive. Not until the Bolshevik Revolution threw America off balance, not until the country began to doubt that the world's future would be transacted in liberal terms, did the United States feel compelled to export its ideological preferences aggressively to a non-democratic world.[55] Much else contributed to the aggressive interventionism of twentieth-century American foreign policy, especially the fear that the domestic economy required predictable foreign markets for goods and capital to work smoothly.[56] But behind the lure of open doors and open markets was the cultural insistence, in the face of radical assertions to the contrary, that liberal America, as far as the world's future was concerned, was not used up.

The travail of the Jeffersonians illustrates several diplomatic patterns associated with this ideology of exceptionalism. Arguably, the United States has always taken itself too seriously—in part because of its liberal mission—and has suffered unnecessarily for it. It has often thought that unwelcome events throughout a complex world were motivated primarily by anti-American design. An inability to make vital distinctions concerning the foreign policies of other nations, especially an inability to distinguish between policies that were anti-American by intent, and policies that happened to discomfit America as a result of larger struggles having little to do with the United States, has often bedeviled American foreign policy. A perceptive Pennsylvanian described the Jeffersonians' international setting this way: "[England and France] are engaged in a conflict upon the point of extermination. The weapons they employ, though they wound us, are only meant for each other. Let us act on that idea, and we may preserve our peace without sacrificing either our honor or our property."[57] The

Jeffersonians could not act on that sensible idea.

Second was the Jeffersonians' inability to acknowledge American self-interest in its relations with the rest of the world. Their social thought held that individual self-interest threatened stable domestic community. In the same vein, national self-interest was somehow incompatible with a stable international order. Hence their exquisite gymnastics to find permissable cover, either legal or moral, for national self-regard. Their efforts were perversely successful in that the Jeffersonians became imprisoned by the logic and decency of their own fictions. Once words had transformed interest into benevolence or justice, policy became seductively simple and devoid of any real danger. And when the world scorned their fictions, the Jeffersonians bitterly rejected the world. This tendency later found its fullest expression in the twentieth-century American vacillation between internationalism and isolationism.

Finally, because the Jeffersonians sanctioned their nation's economic urges with republican decency and international law, they were particularly insensitive to the hard interests of other nations. In their diplomacy with England they were unwilling to compromise on any essential issue. On impressments, for example, James Madison once suggested that a workable compromise might combine an English promise to forego impressments and return Americans already taken, with an American promise to forego employing English sailors and to return those already enticed into the American merchant service. When Albert Gallatin discovered that the return of bona fide English sailors would imperil American commerce because so many of them were in the American service, such a compromise on impressments was never again discussed.[58] On the outstanding commercial issues, a suitable compromise might have involved less English restriction on America's trade in its own produce in exchange for an American willingness to scale down its claims to full carrying privileges because they so clearly complicated England's struggle for national survival. Although this line of action received some attention in 1808 cabinet meetings, it was never seriously pursued.[59]

The desire for complete victory on all essential issues precludes peaceful settlement when the nation's diplomatic adversary has vital interests to protect as well. Admittedly, the Napoleonic Wars imposed a difficult set of problems on the Jeffersonians, as difficult as any faced by American statesmen before the Civil War. Yet the Jeffersonians might have managed their predicament better had they been able to acknowledge the legitimacy and relevance of

England's interests, commitments, and problems. Instead, they saw the worldwide conflict between France and England as only an annoying impediment to the more important global story of American development. Such flawed perception took a heavy toll on the conduct of Republican foreign policy. Unfortunately subsequent American history would provide additional proof that the world is more dangerous when it is poorly understood.

NOTES

1. Garry Wills, *Inventing America: Jefferson's Declaration of Independence* (New York, 1978); Morton White, *The Philosophy of the American Revolution* (New York, 1978); Lance Banning, *The Jeffersonian Persuasion: Evolution of a Party Ideology* (Ithaca, N.Y., 1978); Forrest McDonald, *The Presidency of Thomas Jefferson* (Lawrence, Kan., 1976); Robert M. Johnstone, Jr., *Jefferson and the Presidency: Leadership in the Young Republic* (Ithaca, N.Y., 1978); Noble E. Cunningham, Jr., *The Process of Government Under Jefferson* (Princeton, N.J., 1978); Burton Spivak, *Jefferson's English Crisis: Commerce, Embargo, and the Republican Revolution* (Charlottesville, Va., 1979); Drew R. McCoy, *The Elusive Republic: Political Economy in Jeffersonian America* (Chapel Hill, N.C., 1980); Ralph Lerner, "Commerce and Character: The Anglo-American as New-Model Man," *William and Mary Quarterly*, 3d Ser., XXXVI (1979), pp. 3-26.
2. Jefferson's course in the American imagination has been brilliantly traced by Merrill D. Peterson in *The Jefferson Image in the American Mind* (New York, 1960).
3. The phrase is from David Hawke, *A Transaction of Free Men: The Birth and Course of the Declaration of Independence* (New York, 1964).
4. The beginnings of this market definition of society in the age of Jefferson are suggested in Forrest McDonald, *Alexander Hamilton: A Biography* (New York, 1979), and Morton J. Horwitz, *The Transformation of American Law, 1780-1860* (Cambridge, Mass., 1977).
5. Thomas Jefferson to John Adams, October 16, 1816, in Lester J. Cappon, ed., *The Adams-Jefferson Letters* (Chapel Hill, N.C., 1959), II, 492.
6. Lerner, "Commerce and Character: The Anglo-American as New-Model Man," pp. 3-26.
7. Jefferson to James Ogilvie, August 11, 1811, Jefferson to Horatio G. Spafford, March 17, 1814, in Albert Ellery Bergh, ed., *The Writings of Thomas Jefferson* (Washington, D.C., 1907), XIII, 69; XIV, 120.
8. Jefferson, "A Summary View of the Rights of British North America,"

in Merrill D. Peterson, ed., *The Portable Thomas Jefferson* (New York, 1977), pp. 20-21.

9. *The Anas*, July 8, August 2, 20, 1793, Bergh, *Writings of Jefferson*, I, 366-68, 380-83, 390-93; Jefferson to Colonel Mason, February 4, 1790, Jefferson to James Madison, May 19, 1793, Jefferson to Elbridge Gerry, January 26, 1799, *ibid.*, VIII, 124-25; IX, 97; X, 77; The Autobiography of Thomas Jefferson, *ibid.*, I, 158-59.

10. For recent discussions of this theme see Spivak, *Jefferson's English Crisis*, pp. 1-12, 198-225; McCoy, *The Elusive Republic*, pp. 76-119.

11. The Autobiography of Thomas Jefferson, Bergh, *Writings of Jefferson*, I, 89-90.

12. For a careful analysis of American commercial diplomacy after the Revolution, particularly from Jefferson's vantage point, see Merrill D. Peterson, "Thomas Jefferson and Commercial Policy, 1783-93," in Peterson, ed., *Thomas Jefferson, a Profile* (New York, 1967), pp. 104-34.

13. John Adams to Jefferson, August 7, September 4, November 4, 1785, Julian P. Boyd, ed., *The Papers of Thomas Jefferson* (Princeton, N.J., 1950-), VIII, 354-55; IX, 11.

14. Jefferson to Hogendorp, October 13, 1785, Bergh, *Writings of Jefferson*, V, 184.

15. Spivak, *Jefferson's English Crisis*, pp. x-xi, 68-70.

16. Jefferson to John Jay, August 23, 1785, Bergh, *Writings of Jefferson*, V, 93-95.

17. Jefferson to Benjamin Franklin, August 13, 1774, *ibid.*, IV, 34.

18. Jefferson to David Hartley, July 2, 1787, *ibid.*, VI, 151; Jefferson to John Adams, October 28, 1813, Cappon, *Adams-Jefferson Letters*, II, 388; Jefferson to Madame La Duchesse D'Auville, April 2, 1790, Jefferson to John Dickinson, March 6, 1801, Jefferson to Dr. Joseph Priestly, June 19, 1802, Bergh, *Writings of Jefferson*, VIII, 18; X, 217, 324-25; Autobiography, *ibid.*, I, 158-59; Jefferson to Colonel Mason, February 4, 1790, *ibid.*, VIII, 124-25.

19. The relationship between social milieu, republican character, and political institutions runs through much of Jefferson's writings. Particular aspects of the theme can be traced in Jefferson to Baron Geismer, September 6, 1785, Jefferson to John Bannister, October 15, 1785, Jefferson to James Ross, May 8, 1786, Jefferson to George Washington, November 14, 1786, Jefferson to Benjamin Hawkins, August 4, 1787, Jefferson to Peter Carr, August 10, 1786, Jefferson to Governor Rutledge, August 6, 1787, Jefferson to Mr. M'alister, December 22, 1791, Jefferson to Lafayette, June 16, 1792, Jefferson to Washington, September 9, 1792, Jefferson to John Sullivan, February 9, 1797, Jefferson to John Taylor, June 1, 1798, Jefferson to Thomas Lomas, March 12, 1799, Jefferson to Thaddeus Kosciusko, April 2, 1802, Jefferson to David Williams, November 14, 1803, *ibid.*, V, 128-29, 185-88, 325; VI, 2-4, 251-62; VIII, 274-75, 396-408;

IX, 377-78; X, 44-47, 123-24, 173, 310, 428-31.

20. Jefferson to John Adams, October 16, 1816, Cappon, *Adams-Jefferson Letters*, II, 492; Jefferson to Peter Carr, August 19, 1785, Jefferson to James Madison, June 20, 1787, Jefferson to Washington, August 14, 1787, Jefferson to Peter Carr, August 10, 1787, Jefferson to Thomas Law, June 13, 1814, Bergh, *Writings of Jefferson*, V, 82-87; VI, 134, 256-60, 276-78; XIV, 138-44.

21. Jefferson to John Langdon, September 11, 1785, *ibid.*, V, 131.

22. Jefferson to Mr. Bellini, September 30, 1785, Jefferson to Archibald Stuart, January 25, 1786, Jefferson to Mrs. Bingham, February 7, 1787, Jefferson to Washington, August 14, 1787, Jefferson to William Duane, August 4, 1812, Jefferson to Monsieur Dupont de Nemours, April 24, 1816, *ibid.*, V, 152-54, 259; VI, 81-82, 276-78; XIII, 181-82; XIV, 487-93.

23. Jefferson to Madison, December 12, 1787, Jefferson to Henry Middleton, January 8, 1813, *ibid.*, VI, 392-93; XIII, 203.

24. Jefferson to Wilson Miles Cary, August 12, 1787, Jefferson to Washington, August 14, 1787, Jefferson to John Blair, August 13, 1787, Boyd, *Papers of Jefferson*, XII, 24, 38, 28.

25. For a full treatment of Jefferson's anglophobia see Spivak, *Jefferson's English Crisis*, passim.

26. Jefferson to Abigail Adams, June 21, 1785, Jefferson to John Adams, February 28, 1796, Cappon, *Adams-Jefferson Letters*, I, 34, 200.

27. Jefferson to Dr. Price, August 7, 1785, Bergh, *Writings of Jefferson*, V, 57; Wills, *Inventing America*, pp. 273-319, 374-79.

28. Jefferson to Madison, March 19, 1803, James Madison Papers, Library of Congress, Ser. 2, Reel 25.

29. *The Anas*, March 1, July 10, October 1, 1792, February 7, March 2, 1793, Bergh, *Writings of Jefferson*, I, 271-83, 290-92, 309-12, 316-19, 332-33, 345; Jefferson to Washington, May 23, 1792, Jefferson to Phillip Mazei, April 24, 1796, Jefferson to Elbridge Gerry, May 13, 1797, Jefferson to General Gates, May 30, 1797, Jefferson to Colonel Arthur Campbell, September 1, 1797, Jefferson to A. H. Rowan, September 26, 1798, Jefferson to Benjamin Rush, January 16, 1811, *ibid.*, VIII, 342-49; IX, 336, 383-85, 391-92, 419-20; X, 60; XIII, 4; Spivak, *Jefferson's English Crisis*, pp. 210-20. Federalism, Jefferson wrote in 1797, was "calculated to sap the very found tions of republicanism." See Jefferson to Aaron Burr, July 17, 1797, Bergh, *Writings of Jefferson*, IX, 403.

30. Jefferson to General Henry Dearborn, August 14, 1811, Jefferson to William A. Burwell, August 19, 1811, *ibid.*, XIII, 73, 78; Jefferson to John Langdon, September 11, 1785, Jefferson to Richard Henry Lee, April 22, 1786, Jefferson to John Page, May 4, 1786, Jefferson to William Carmichael, May 5, 1786, Jefferson to Edward Rutledge, July 4, 1790, August 25, 1791, Jefferson to John Hollins, May 11,

1811, Jefferson to John Crawford, January 2, 1812, *ibid.,* V, 130-31, 292-94, 305-06, 308; VIII, 60, 234; XIII, 58, 118; Jefferson to John Adams, September 24, November 19, 1785, Jefferson to Abigail Adams, August 9, 1786, Cappon, *Adams-Jefferson Letters,* I, 68, 94-96, 149.

31. Jefferson to James Monroe, July 17, 1785, Jefferson to Elbridge Gerry, May 17, 1786, Jefferson to Colonel Humphreys, May 7, 1786, Jefferson to Colonel Innes, March 13, 1791, Jefferson to Thomas Pinckney, June 11, 1792, Jefferson to Madison, March, 1793, Bergh, *Writings of Jefferson,* V, 16-20, 315-16, 319; VIII, 145-46, 369-72; IX, 33-34.

32. Jefferson to Lafayette, November 3, 1786, Boyd, *Papers of Jefferson,* X, 505.

33. Benjamin Stoddert to Jefferson, January 25, 1809, Thomas Jefferson Papers Library of Congress.

34. Jefferson to John Blair, August 13, 1787, Jefferson to Washington, August 14, 1787, Boyd, *Papers of Jefferson,* XII, 28, 38; Jefferson to John Jay, October 8, 1787, Jefferson to William Short, October 3, 1801, Bergh, *Writings of Jefferson,* VI, 323-34; X, 285-88.

35. Jefferson to Pierre Samuel Dupont de Nemours, February 12, 1806, Jefferson Papers.

36. Jefferson to James Bowdoin, July 10, 1806, *ibid.*

37. This and the following paragraph builds from Spivak, *Jefferson's English Crisis,* pp. 15-25.

38. John Randolph in *Annals,* 9th Cong., 1st Sess., pp. 555-74, 591-605.

39. John Taylor to Madison, January 15, 1808, Madison Papers, University of Virginia.

40. Jefferson's long effort to multiply America's sources of industrial supply was connected to his realization that without such economic diversity nonimportation was a useless foreign policy weapon. Its utility was always predicated on an array of trading partners because without such diversity, closing the American market to England, regardless of justification, would become fiscally dangerous, given the importance of import duties to government revenues and the retirement of the public debt. Throughout Jefferson's second term, leading Republicans realized that England's near monopoly over American imports denied nonimportation a role in Anglo-American commercial dealings. Senator Samuel Smith of Maryland recognized the problem: "It is indeed a mortifying thing that we cannot in an effectual manner resist the insults and injuries of G[reat] B[ritain]. . . . We have no revenue but that arises from importation. We have eight million dollars annually to pay for the extinguishment of the public debt and the interest thereon besides all the expenditures of government, the army and navy. If by nonimportation we cut off that great source of revenue, how are we to meet the payment?" See Samuel

Smith to [?], December 19, 1805, Samuel Smith Letterbooks, Samuel Smith Papers, Library of Congress.
41. Randolph's words are quoted in Merrill D. Peterson, *Thomas Jefferson and the New Nation* (New York, 1970), p. 829.
42. Jefferson to Albert Gallatin, December 15, 1807, Jefferson to Gideon Granger, January 22, 1808, Jefferson to William Cabell, March 13, 1808, Jefferson Papers; Nathaniel Macon to Joseph Hooper Nicholson, February 20, 1808, Joseph Hooper Nicholson Papers, Library of Congress; *American State Papers: Foreign Relations*, III, 25-26; Dumas Malone, *Jefferson the President: Second Term, 1805-1809* (Boston, 1974), p. 481.
43. Jefferson to Madison, March 11, 1808, Jefferson Papers.
44. For a full treatment of the embargo's relationship to war see Spivak, *Jefferson's English Crisis*, pp. 103-36.
45. Madison to William Pinkney, July 18, 1808, Madison to John Armstrong, July 18, 1808, Diplomatic Instructions, All Countries, vol. 7, National Archives.
46. Jefferson to Robert Livingston, October 15, 1808, Jefferson Papers.
47. Madison to Armstrong, May 2, 1808, Diplomatic Instructions, All Countries, vol. 6, National Archives.
48. William Pinkney to Madison, December 25, 1808, Dispatches, Great Britain, vol. 15, National Archives; Madison to Armstrong, July 22, 1808, Diplomatic Instructions, All Countries, vol. 6, National Archives.
49. Orchard Cook to John Quincy Adams, January 1, 1809, Adams Family Papers, Massachusetts Historical Society, Boston, Reel 407.
50. Jefferson to Thomas Leiper, January 21, 1809, Jefferson to David Humphreys, January 20, 1809, Jefferson to Benjamin Stoddert, February 18, 1809, Jefferson Papers; C. P. Sumner to Joseph Story, December, 1808, Joseph Story Papers, Library of Congress; Jefferson to Monsieur Dupont de Nemours, April 15, 1811, Jefferson to John Adams, January 21, 1812, Jefferson to General Thaddeus Kosciusko, June 28, 1812, Jefferson to John Melish, January 13, 1813, Jefferson to James Maury, June 16, 1815, Jefferson to Benjamin Austin, January 9, 1816, Bergh, *Writings of Jefferson*, XIII, 38-39, 122-24, 170-71, 207-08; XIV, 315-19, 388-92; Spivak, *Jefferson's English Crisis*, pp. 203-10.
51. Jefferson to Monroe, May 5, 1811, Jefferson to Baron Alexander von Humbolt, December 6, 1813, Jefferson to John Crawford, January 2, 1814, Jefferson to Thaddeus Kosciusko, April 13, 1814, Bergh, *Writings of Jefferson*, XIII, 60, 117-19; XIV, 22, 41-43; Jefferson to John Adams, August 10, 1815, Cappon, *Adams-Jefferson Letters*, II, 454.
52. Jefferson to John Adams, June 10, 1815, *ibid.*, 442-43; Jefferson to Thomas Cooper, January 16, 1814, Bergh, *Writings of Jefferson*, XIV, 54-63.
53. N. Gordon Levin organizes much of his fine book, *Woodrow Wilson*

and World Politics: America's Response to War and Revolution (New York, 1968) around the theme of exceptionalism.

54. The best treatment of America's continental expansion is still Norman A. Graebner, *Empire on the Pacific* (New York, 1955).

55. Levin, *Wilson and World Politics,* pp. 254-60.

56. See Walter LaFeber, *The New Empire: An Interpretation of American Expansion, 1860-1898* (Ithaca, N.Y., 1963).

57. Alexander Dallas to Albert Gallatin, December 23, 1807, Albert Gallatin Papers, New York University, Reel 15.

58. James Madison, Observations in Cabinet Meeting, February 2, 1807, Jefferson Papers; Gallatin to Madison, April 13, 1807, Jefferson to Madison, April 21, 1807, Madison Papers, Library of Congress, Ser. 2, Reel 25.

59. Jefferson, Notes on Cabinet Meeting, July 6, 1808, Jefferson Papers.

3

JAMES MADISON, FOREIGN POLICY, AND THE UNION

Robert A. Rutland

James Madison was perhaps unique among the Founding Fathers in that he judged all political considerations, including foreign policy, as either strengthening or weakening the Republic. Slavery was an evil, but mainly because it created a threat to the Union. And slavery was, despite its implications for foreign policy, an *internal* problem—it was something the American people had to settle by themselves. On the other hand, most of the political questions Madison faced throughout his career were intertwined with foreign relations. Even in such ostensibly domestic matters as ratifying the Constitution, foreign policy considerations were never far from Madison's mind. American foreign policy was Madison's chief concern for sixteen crucial years in the nation's history. Indeed, his successes and failures have led to a curious judgment on Madison's stature as a leader. The early Madison—the Founding Father of the Republic and cofounder of the Democratic-Republican party—is adjudged successful. But Madison the secretary of state and president has received lower marks from historians. One recent writer alluded to Madison as "an inept manager of men"; another depicted him as a man "not endowed with political insight, wisdom, or art"; and Henry Adams saw Madison as a secretary of state whose "measures and conduct toward Europe showed the habit of avoiding the heart of every issue, in order to fret its extremities," traits which "led him into his chief difficulties at home and abroad."[1]

Madison's preparation for his post as secretary of state in Jefferson's cabinet had been on-the-job training as a congressman. From the vantage point of a Virginia delegate he had seen the Spaniards threaten commerce on the Mississippi and knew both Spain and England had tried to undermine the loyalty of Kentuckians toward the Union. Then he had learned with regret that his New England friends were more interested in selling codfish to Spain than in keeping alive the spirit of Unionism in the West.

As for England, Madison came by his Anglophobia naturally. Surely he heard Jefferson tell of his snubbing at George III's court and knew the long-prevailing sentiment in England that America would in time be forced to beg for readmission to the British Empire.[2] Thereafter, Madison did not need to believe that Shawnee scalping knives bore a Manchester trademark to feel hostile toward England. The seizure of American vessels by the British navy after November 1793 and the impressment of American seamen on the ground that they were in fact British deserters rankled in Madison's breast and made him one of the most outspoken critics of normal relations with Great Britain in the ensuing session of Congress. More on this later, but suffice it to say here that throughout his public life Madison complained that he was constantly confronted with instances of British "insults and aggressions without a parallel in the history of the world; we have seen our neutrality violated, ourselves insulted, and our national sovereignty attacked."[3] From the beginning of the nation's existence Great Britain was the *bête noire* of American foreign policy. Certainly James Madison was never allowed to forget it.

President Jefferson tried to put aside past instances of British aggression when he promised in his inaugural address to seek "honest friendship, with all nations—entangling alliances with none." This principle, echoing Washington's famous dictum, sounded good in the abstract. However, Madison had to deal with the realities of a world where two major powers, England and France, had mobilized their economic and human resources toward the total destruction of each other's armies and navies. As early as 1793 the British minister to the United States pointed out that "The distress results from the unusual mode of war employed by the enemy himself, in having armed almost the whole laboring class of the French nation, for the purpose of commencing and supporting hostilities against all the governments of Europe."[4] The limited wars of the eighteenth century became a thing of the past, and neutral rights, never secure, were further jeopardized in a new era of total war.

In such circumstances, Madison's tenure as secretary of state (1801-1809) was marked by persistent but eventually unsuccessful efforts to gain recognition of American maritime rights as a neutral power. After an early and relatively calm period when American shipping flourished during a brief peaceful interval, the whole question of neutrality (with its concomitant problems of impressment, seized ships, and confiscated cargoes) was forced upon the Jefferson administration. Here was a President committed to a reduction of the public debt, with drastic cutbacks in military and naval expenditures assumed by his Republican partisans. Jefferson kept his promises, and thus Madison was forced to deal from a weakened position as he attempted negotiations for the American claim that neutral ships carry neutral goods. Neither the British nor the French agreed. After struggling for a decade, Madison finally decided that some problems in foreign affairs can only be solved by a declaration of war.

Before Madison's patience ran out, his duties as head of the copyright and patent offices, keeper of the great seal, archivist, and publisher of the public laws eventually became incidental to the main business of keeping American ships safe on the high seas. Without a navy that could enforce public policy, it proved to be an impossible task. Nonetheless, Jefferson and Madison spoke of foreign affairs almost every day until March 3, 1809, with their unrecorded conversations leading to a variety of actions that barely kept the young nation out of war. The price, however, was high in the loss of national esteem and even higher in the loss of American seamen and crippled international commerce.

Madison and Jefferson worked so closely together, and their concepts of foreign policy were so harmonious, that it is difficult to isolate the secretary of state's personal influence on diplomacy. Yet, unlike Madison, Jefferson had served as a diplomat in Europe and matched Madison's devotion to the Union with a personal contempt for aristocracy and monarchy. Jefferson spoke of war often but dreaded the expense and uncertainty of armed conflict. As president he valued Madison's advice and more than once gave testimonials to his admiration of his younger colleague's abilities. He once told Benjamin Rush he considered Madison "the greatest man in the world" and as early as 1794 hinted to Madison that he might someday become president.[5] In the aftermath of the bitter quarrel over the Jay treaty, the loose political reins were gathered in their hands and they worked as a team to form a cohesive political party. The new Republican party was avowedly pro-French and in time would be more than a match for the pro-British Federalists (or Jacobins and Monocrats, as their enemies said). For the rest of their lives, Jefferson and Madison disdained "high-flying monarchy men" and sought to keep them out of public office.

In the exuberant days of 1789, Jefferson and Madison regarded the French Revolution as a European manifestation of their own, and when the liberty cap went askew they were reluctant to condemn French excesses. Had not Jefferson himself spoken of bloodletting as a way of fertilizing the tree of liberty? The rise of Napoleon placed a different face on French affairs, however, so that the Republican leaders grew to distrust the bellicose hero whose wars and plunder represented a betrayal of revolutionary goals. Alarmed at the open Anglophilism of Federalist leaders, particularly men of wealth living above the Hudson River, the two Virginians worked together to oppose such excesses as the Alien and Sedition laws or the Federalists' attempt to imitate British models of ministerial government financed by excises on domestic manufactures, a central bank, and a permanent public debt. To reverse such a program Republicans confidently appealed to tillers of the soil as the only safe guardians of the Republic's future. In a country with a population that was 85 percent agrarian, their appeal was broad and their smashing election victory in 1800 was foreordained.

II

Jefferson brought Madison into the cabinet as his chief lieutenant. Although Madison bore the title of secretary of state, he was in fact the presidential alter ego whose thinking was nearly always attuned to Jefferson's. No less than other national leaders both men had read widely in Grotius, Vattel, Burlamaqui, and other writers on international and natural law and believed that republics flourished best in times of peace. Jefferson did what he could to dismantle the domestic Federalist program he inherited but was content with John Adams's accomplishments in foreign affairs. The quasi-war with France ended with concessions from the French, and with the return of peace in Europe Jefferson took pains to assure the British that the last thing he sought was a quarrel with the mother country.[6] Jefferson in fact hoped to have England in a friendly posture if his plan to acquire New Orleans and the Floridas from Spain could materialize. The extraordinary series of events which culminated in the Louisiana Purchase depended more on Napoleon's cupidity than on any scheme worked out in Washington, but this major achievement of Jefferson's administration was carried off with the benign indifference of the British ministry and indeed with the financial intervention of a leading London banking firm. The British profited from their enemy even as they worked to defeat him on the battlefield. French troops fought in uniforms made from British cloth, and Whitehall tacitly allowed Napoleon to acquire money for cranking up his war machine from London sources.

The British soon made up for that oversight. Knowing that Napoleon meant to subjugate Great Britain, the British revived a series of trade orders and naval restrictions that inevitably brought clashes with American interests on the high seas. Anticipating further trouble on the impressment issue, Madison told the American minister in London to make it clear how such actions "exasperate the feelings of this Country." The British were to expect that concessions on impressment "will doubtless be insisted on by this Country, in case of a renewal of the war, or whenever another war shall take place."[7] At that time, the total number of seamen impressed from American ships was less than 2,500, and the number had dropped sharply during the Franco-British armistice.[8]

In the afterglow of the Louisiana triumph, Jefferson left the galling impressment problem in Madison's hands. Stung by a realization that a sovereign nation cannot permit the boarding of its vessels and the manhandling of their crews without feelings of shame, Madison accordingly sent to the new American minister in London, James Monroe, a proposed convention which pledged the two nations to stop impressments, defined munitions as cargoes which could not "be excepted from the freedom of the neutral flag," and prohibited "paper blockades."[9] As Britain swung her navy into action, the tension caused by impressments mounted. The impressment issue was not a factor in the reelection of Jefferson in 1804, however, and in his second inaugural address the president spoke at length about the newspaper attacks upon his administration while he ignored impressment completely.

The honeymoon was soon over. An important British book, assailing the idea of maritime neutrality (James Stephen's *War in Disguise*), influenced Parliament as Napoleon's armies marched across Europe; the *Essex* decision in a British court upset the old practice of allowing American ships to carry French colonial products; and Nelson's victory at Trafalgar established Britain's mastery of the seas. The British navy renewed with vigor its impressment policy while Monroe tried to talk about the problem with the British foreign secretary. Then in May, 1806, the British cabinet issued a new series of orders in council as a means of strangling Napoleon's economic program. The clear message to Madison was that England was still treating the United States as little more than a British dependency. A popular British work unabashedly proclaimed that English policy ought to render "the foreign trade of the whole world subservient to the increase of her shipping and navigation."[10] The maddening arrogance of the British forced Madison into a scholarly retreat. He spent days doing research in the standard works on neutrality in international law, and laboriously penned a 70,000-word treatise titled *Examination of the British Doctrine, which subjects to capture a Neutral Trade Not Open in Time of Peace.* Although the work proved Madison could handle the scholarly side of international law well, its pedantic tone and great length made it a weak diplomatic weapon. Congressman John Randolph dismissed the performance with a wave of the hand as "a shilling pamphlet hurled against eight hundred ships of war."[11]

Looking back, the *Essex* decision in 1805 reviving the Rule of 1756 (which denied to neutral flags a commerce in war which was prohibited in peace) set the two nations on a war course, because the British gained too much and the Americans lost both profit and honor. For a time the British had more or less suspended the rule as American ship captains learned how to evade it by carrying French or Spanish Caribbean produce to an American port, picking up new ship's papers which neutralized the cargoes, which were then sent to a European port. Now the British court declared the "broken voyage" a fiction; this made American ships fair game for confiscation and sale as prizes of war. Once he heard this news, Madison guessed that "a dreadful scene of distress may ensue on our commerce" and predicted that unless England withdrew the new ruling "absolute submission, or some other resort in vindication of our neutral rights, will be the only alternative left."[12]

Busy shipyards, a forest of masts in crowded harbors, and bustling warehouses told another story. Cotton at Charleston in 1805 sold at an all-time high price of 51.6 cents a pound, with nearly nine million pounds exported that year. Corn prices in Virginia shot from 61 cents per bushel in 1801 to 94 cents in 1805.

Wheat rose from 98 cents a bushel in 1802 to $1.46 in 1804.[13] The foundations of this Republican prosperity were jeopardized by the British naval pincers that sent insurance rates soaring and seemed to make a mockery of American neutrality. Faced with a crisis, as biographer Harold Schultz noted, Madison was inclined to apply the political solutions of the 1790s to contemporary problems.[14] Economic sanctions had brought England to her senses in the Stamp Act emergency of 1765, when Madison was only a boy. As a congressman he persistently sought a discriminatory tax against British goods, and in 1794 he also advocated the peaceable weaponry of embargo and nonimportation as retaliatory steps, forced by British seizures of American ships in the West Indies. John Adams's casting vote in the Senate defeated the plan, but Madison never doubted the trustworthiness of economic retaliation, and he revived the notion in 1805 when England reacted hysterically to Napoleon's land victories. "If force should be necessary on our part it can in no way be so justly or usefully employed as in maintaining the status quo," Madison advised the vacationing president. "The efficacy of an embargo also cannot be doubted."[15] Congress responded with a Nonimportation Act meant to strengthen the hands of American negotiators in London.

Jefferson was not as consistent in his thinking. At one time he considered an alliance with England, but he later backed off and spoke again of the need to avoid foreign entanglements. Then Monroe and Pinkney negotiated a treaty with the British Foreign Office that offered only an inconclusive statement on impressment, ignored American spoliation claims, but made real concessions on the re-export trade with Caribbean colonies. In the midst of these negotiations Napoleon issued his Berlin Decree, which threw a "paper blockade" around Great Britain and thus made any neutral ship or cargo bound for the islands fair game for French privateers. Meanwhile, Jefferson sent word to London that the cessation of impressment was a sina qua non, and he suspended judgment when the preliminary draft reached Washington. Madison warned the American negotiators that "in refusing an explicit pledge agst. the horrible practice of impressments" the British were seeking what America could not give.[16] When it was obvious that England would not yield another inch on impressments, Jefferson simply threw the treaty into the wastebasket as too contemptible to deserve submission to the Senate for ratification.

As newspapers in Boston and New York continued to report more ships seized by the British navy, anxious merchants worried about cargoes in the Mediterranean claimed as prizes by French and Spanish privateers. Resisting pressure for costly enlargement of the navy, Jefferson opted instead (and presumably after consulting Madison) for a frugal defensive policy calling for the construction of gunboats to cruise shorelines and harbors. The Nonimportation Act of 1806 was a dead letter, and in the cabinet realists such as Albert Gallatin were inclined to speak of the choices narrowing to either a tightly enforced embargo or a declaration of war on England or France or both. In short, if the war in Europe continued, the United States would have to either close its harbors to international commerce or fight an expensive war to assert the rights of neutral powers to use every sea lane around the globe. Yet Madison confronted the dilemma that either alternative would surely arouse opposition in Federalist New England and thereby undermine the Union that he sought to preserve.

Vexation with international diplomacy was one thing; killing of American sailors was another—and far more intolerable. Thus the nation was electrified by the news in June, 1807, that the British frigate *Leopard* had attacked the *Chesapeake* practically within sight of the American coastline. The country would have responded to a presidential war message with alacrity, but Jefferson chose instead to await a reaction from the British cabinet. Reparations for families of the dead and punishment for the responsible naval officer were slow in coming, but the Republican principle of legislative supremacy shared by Madison and Jefferson held that Congress ought to make the decision if war was to come. Meanwhile, the British seemed bent on pushing American patience to the limit. "Even a Revenue Cutter conveying the Vice President and his sick daughter from Washington to New York and wearing her distinctive and well known colours did not escape insult," Madison told Monroe. The American envoy in London was also informed of the sweep made by a British squadron into the Chesapeake Bay virtually to blockade the port of Norfolk. "These enormities superadded to all that have gone before . . . form a mass of injuries and provocations which have justly excited the indignant feelings of the nation and severely tried the patience of the Government," Madison added.[17] Monroe protested, but Whitehall was not impressed. What were the lives of three American sailors, when the fate of Europe and the British Empire was suspended by a thread and Napoleon was running rampant on the continent?

A special session of Congress had no better answer than the president and the secretary of state when it convened in October

1807. The written records are skimpy but no doubt Jefferson conversed with Madison hour after hour, reviewing the events from 1793 onward. For a time American shipping had enjoyed an unprecedented wave of prosperity (even farmers shared in the profits) as the European powers grappled with one another in a new kind of warfare involving massed armies, ravaged fields, neglected produce, and hungry people everywhere. American grain, fish, tobacco, and naval stores found a ready market until the British and French both fashioned vises of their own, aimed at sweeping neutrals from the oceans. American policy still affirmed "free ships, free goods," but the principle fell on deaf British ears, and a series of court rulings and orders in council tightened the blockade of continental Europe. Another British order in council (November 11, 1807) was full of impudence, for it allowed neutral ships to trade at ports barred to British ships provided the vessels first cleared at an English port and paid the king's agents duties on the cargo! In short, Americans could trade with France if they called at a British port first, paid imposts, and obtained a royal license. If they failed to follow these directions, American ships were subject to British capture and sale.

All neutral shipping was affected, but ships flying the American colors were the most obvious target of the latest orders. Indeed, Americans asked themselves, if such rules could be made in London and enforced on every Yankee ship in European waters, who actually had won the American Revolution? British policy since 1783 in nearly every respect, from the first occupation of Western outposts down to this latest outrage, seemed directed at keeping America in the status of a subservient dependency. Napoleon's Milan Decree retaliated by declaring United States ships that complied with the orders in council would be subject to French seizure. There was no direction for American firms to turn without risking total loss of ship and crew.

III

In such circumstances, Jefferson and Madison decided that an embargo was the only alternative to war. A war against both France and England they rejected as impracticable. A war with England was appealing to some Republicans who thought Canada was there for the taking. Albert Gallatin, the secretary of the treasury, was hardheaded and realistic. "I prefer war to a permanent embargo," Gallatin told the president.[18] Congress took the bait Jefferson offered in a special message and speedily enacted the Embargo. Madison and Jefferson saw the law as a means of buying time: either the war would end or the belligerents would see their error and correct it. Until England and France recognized "some sense of *moral duty*," Jefferson noted, "we keep within ourselves. This gives time, time may produce peace in Europe: peace in Europe removes all causes of difference."[19] The hope that the British would recognize neutral rights proved to be wishful thinking, and for more than a century they declined to endorse the principle of freedom of the seas during wartime.

Diplomacy based on hope and good intentions has rarely served the long-term interests of the United States, but Madison considered war as the single alternative to an embargo and he preferred exhausting every means of preserving peace. Some years earlier Madison had decided "that war should be the last resort of all countries with republican institutions," and he had not changed his mind in 1808. He still believed that wars brought armies, armies brought debts and taxes, "and armies, and debts, and taxes, are the known instruments for bringing the many under the domination of the few." Madison extended his warning:

> In war, too, the discretionary power of the Executive is extended; its influence in dealing out offices, honors, and emoluments is multiplied; and all the means of seducing the minds, are added to those of subduing the force, of the people.[20]

Thus Madison practiced forbearance in the face of continued British hostility and Napoleonic ambition.

New England reacted to the Embargo first with a surly shrug and then with outright defiance of federal officers attempting to enforce the law. Madison was appalled that Americans would traffic with the British. He conceded that smuggling took place as he tried to explain to the American minister in London that the Embargo would force the British to realize the futility of their harsh policy. "The sense of Natl. honor & independence seems to be entering deeper & deeper into the mass of the people," he reported.[21] Alas, Madison was deluding himself, for the widespread unemployment and falling commodity prices could not be whistled away.

How one portion of the Union could be so disaffected, placing smuggling profits above patriotism, mystified Madison. American foreign policy was aimed at making the profits of New England shippers legitimate, not gains through underhanded methods that amounted to trading with a hostile nation. In his bewilderment Madison told a Massachusetts congressman, "All we contend for is principally the interests of the north—the carrying trade in particular."[22] Passage of the Enforcement Act, clearly aimed at harsh punishment for smugglers defying the Embargo, brought contemptuous resistance from the legislatures in Connecticut and Massachusetts. The seeds of the Hartford convention were broadcast on New England's rocky soil during the winter of 1808–1809 as disappointed Federalists realized one Virginian would succeed another in the White House.

Pressure to repeal the Embargo become irresistible in the final hours of Jefferson's second term, yet Madison retained his belief that economic retaliation was the best weapon a morally upright republican government could wield in the worsening crisis. When his election as President was beyond doubt, Madison reaffirmed his faith in the Embargo. "It can not I think be doubted that if the Embargo be repealed & the orders be enforced," he told Pinkney, "that war is inevitable."[23] To the end of his tenure as secretary of state, Madison entertained no doubts about the efficacy of economic sanctions as a republican alternative to war.

The bonds of union had been severely strained by the Embargo. The American export trade fell from $108.3 million in 1807 to $22.4 million in 1808.[24] New England resisted the law and threatened defiance until repeal ended the Republican gamble on the day Jefferson retired from the White House. Madison still played for time, hoping as Jefferson had hoped that the European war would somehow end and dissolve all the problems afflicting American commerce. Finally, time ran out.

Except for the Louisiana Purchase, which was not his triumph but Jefferson's, Madison had little to show for his weary eight years as secretary of state. The Republican formula of liberty, frugality, and neutrality had not produced results.[25] The British continued to impress American seamen, American ships were condemned in the prize courts of France and England, and the Floridas were still under the Spanish flag. Anxious to avoid the expense of a larger navy, however, Madison favored an old-fashioned isolationist policy that called for more hardship than the American business community was willing to bear.

As a chief architect of the Embargo, Madison must bear some of the blame for the shambles that Jefferson's administration became during its last four months in office. The only way to pick up the pieces and keep the Union intact, Madison reluctantly concluded, was to force England to rescind the orders in council or go to war. War, however, was the last thing Madison wanted. "War contains so much folly, as well as wickedness, that much is to be hoped from the progress of reason," Madison observed during his days in Congress, "and if any thing is to be hoped, everything ought to be tried."[26] Consistent and rational himself, now Madison's turn came to deal with the British when in March 1809 he moved into the President's House.

IV

Madison hoped the people would be with him, whatever happened. He read with unusual interest the many resolutions sent him by city and county meetings of ardent citizens who pledged their support to the new administration. Typical were those from Washington County, Maryland, where the assembled Republicans praised the purposes of the Embargo, promised Madison their support, and offered to fight for national honor if necessary: "Although we deprecate *War* as a great national evil, yet we do believe [sic] the time is near at hand, when it will be necessary to resort to *War*, in order to avoid the greater evil — *of submission to the mandates of Foreign Despots*." While most of these proofs of public approbation came from west and south of the Hudson, Madison wanted to think they reflected a national consensus. "It is highly agreeable to find in these proceedings our national embarrassments traced to their true source," the president replied to one such meeting, "in the injustice and aggressions of foreign powers; and equally so to see the measures for counteracting them so entirely approved."[27] If Congress would only reflect public opinion and eschew petty factionalism, so the reasoning ran, Madison's administration could embark on a course that would bring England and France around to a recognition of the young republic's rights as a neutral in their worldwide struggle.

Such an ideal solution was not to be. Instead of cooperation from prominent Republicans in the Senate, Madison found himself badgered by William Branch Giles of Virginia and Samuel Smith of Maryland — among others — who thwarted the president's cabinet plans and thus handicapped the administration from the outset. Denied the services of able Albert Gallatin in the State Department, Madison settled for the lackluster Robert Smith (brother of the Maryland senator) and eventually found himself answering Smith's mail. With the Embargo a dead letter, Congress bestirred itself with great reluctance by passing the Non-Intercourse Act shortly after Madison's inaugural ball. Clearly a stopgap measure, Madison noted the law "seems to be as little satisfactory out of doors, as it was within."[28] Commerce with Britain and France was forbidden by the act, but trade would be restored if either belligerent recognized American neutrality and honored it on the high seas. The carrot thus dangled before the British cabinet and Napoleon was to be withdrawn at the end of the May session of Congress. Time was working against such an early solution unless Madison proved to be luckier than Jefferson in transAtlantic dealings.

Most of the American resentment was directed toward the despised Orders in Council, a British device which sanctioned naval blockades of enemy ports. Enforced by the Royal Navy, the resulting blows to American commerce and the impressment of American seamen created grievances Madison realized the nation could not tolerate interminably. Then Madison suddenly was offered nearly everything he wanted. The British minister in Washington, David Erskine, had told his superior in London that the president would gladly impose sanctions against French commerce if only the Orders in Council could be removed. Erskine accepted George Canning's reply, which promised to withdraw the Orders if America would keep pressure on France and allow the British Navy to intercept U.S. ships attempting an illegal trade with continental ports, but twisted it. A quick exchange of notes between Erskine and Robert Smith brought an elated Madison to the presidential desk, where he signed a proclamation restoring commerce with England in return for Erskine's assurance that the Orders in Council would be withdrawn on June 10, 1809.[29]

A temporary euphoria struck America, only to dissolve in late July when word reached the New World of the British cabinet's disavowal of the Erskine agreement. Madison was embarrassed and angered by turns as he considered the alternatives he now faced. His summer vacation interrupted by "the mortifying necessity of setting out tomorrow morning for Washington," Madison told Jefferson the fiasco was the result of the "the mixture of fraud & folly" in the British cabinet.[30] What followed only piled insult on to injury, as Erskine was recalled and replaced by a haughty minor British diplomat who soon alienated Madison by implying that the president had known Erskine violated his instructions. Madison took great affront at the suggestion, and agreed with Gallatin that the mere notion that America might allow the Royal Navy to enforce its laws on the high seas was intolerable.

Francis J. Jackson came to Washington as GeorgeIII's emissary that fall, but his tenure in Washington was brief. After an exchange of notes that almost descended to mutual insult, Madison declared Jackson *persona non grata*. Madison had been in office less than a year and had seen his foreign policy gyrate in runaway fashion. Henceforth, Madison left the business of foreign affairs more and more in the incompetent hands of congressmen who spent more time worrying about postmasterships than affairs of state.

Madison tried to resort to diplomacy by authorizing the American envoy in London to negotiate for a relaxation of Britain's hard-line position on neutral commerce. Ultimately, William Pinkney confessed that he was wasting his time and government money by trying to dent the adamant British position. Meanwhile, Congress, in the spring of 1810, stumbled into the enactment of Macon's Bill No. 2, which provided that if either Britain or France revoked its restrictive edicts before March 3, 1811, and the other nation did not respond in similar manner, then non-intercourse regulations would be imposed on the errant power. Napoleon had responded to the Orders in Council with his own Berlin and Milan decrees, which declared a paper blockade of Great Britain with dire penalties for any neutral vessel touching British ports or allowing a search by the British navy. Scores of American vessels, including the merchantman *Jefferson,* had been seized and sold as prizes of war in French ports. On the surface, Macon's Bill No. 2 seemed more to British than French liking since the Royal Navy controlled the ocean. "On the other hand," Madison wrote Jefferson, "this very inequality, which France would confirm by a state of hostilities with the United States, may become a motive with her to turn the tables on G. Britain, by compelling her either to revoke her orders, or to lose the commerce of this country."

Napoleon decided "to turn the tables" by announcing that the Berlin and Milan decrees were being withdrawn. Actually, nothing much was done to see that the obnoxious decrees were revoked, but in diplomatic channels the deed was done. Madison chose to take Napoleon at his word, thereby forcing the British to follow suit or suffer a lowering of the trade barrier against them as provided by Macon's Bill No. 2. The British saw through Napoleon's ploy and demanded proof that France was dealing honestly with the Americans, but Madison chose to treat the French announcement as a *fait accompli.* Loathe to give up their blockade of

European ports, the British stalled until Pinkney packed his bags and Madison cut off all commercial relations between Great Britain and America.

For the next year and a half the French pretended that they were now friendly observers of American neutral commerce while the British sought to convince Americans that they were fighting a continental tyrant on behalf of free nations everywhere. These diplomatic protests of innocence failed to cover up the continued impressment of American seamen by the British navy or the confiscation of American ships and cargoes wherever the Royal Navy operated. Madison's irritation increased, prodded in part by the behavior in Congress of younger men who revived the slogans of 1776. Henry Clay set the record straight as to whether America's chief obstruction to commercial freedom was France or England. "We are invited, conjured, to drink the potion of British poison, actually presented to our lips," Clay said, "that we may avoid the imperial dose prepared by perturbed imaginations. We are called upon to submit to debasement, dishonor and disgrace; to bow the neck to royal insolence, as a course of preparation for manly resistance to gallic invasion! What nation, what individual, was ever taught, in the schools of ignominious submission, the patriot lessons of freedom and independence?"[32]

America was inching toward war, not really wanting it, but willing to fight if either Britain or France chose to ignore the sovereign rights of the United States. Madison had all the provocation needed for a war message when he blundered into the Henry-Crillon affair and wound up paying $50,000 to an alleged British spy (and a fellow imposter) for worthless documents that supposedly proved British complicity in a disunion plot.[33] As the details came out, Madison was mightily embarrassed by his naivete but pretended he had another trump card to play against England. By early April, 1812, he told Jefferson: "It appears that [Spencer] Percival, & c, are to retain their places, and that they prefer war with us, to a repeal of their Orders in Council." Clearly, Madison's patience was exhausted. Even though the nation was ill-prepared for war and the treasury was far from full, the president realized that public opinion had outdistanced him—that the country preferred a fight to continued insults. If the American flag on a mast was worth no more than a dishrag, the American people wanted to know it.

Still, Madison hesitated to send a war message to Congress. Almost all the evidence was in, but Madison and the country awaited a final confirmation of British and French perfidy. The messenger ship, *Hornet,* was due to return early in the spring of 1812. On May 22, 1812, the *Hornet* slipped into an American harbor bearing no news of importance. Nothing had changed. "The business is become more than ever puzzling," Madison admitted to Jefferson, but in truth the president was now about to become isolated from public opinion unless he acted.[35] Where would New England stand? Holding the Union together was always upmost in Madison's mind, so when Massachusetts governor Elbridge Gerry told the President, "By war we shall be purified as by fire," the last glimmer of hope for peace faded. On June 1, 1812, Madison's message to Congress asked for a declaration of war.

Thus war came. One of Madison's few consolations during the gray days that followed came from New England, where former president John Adams kept his vigil. As pro-British Federalists in New England applauded American defeats, Adams asked Madison to make judicious appointments so that "this disaffected Part of the Nation may be gradually reconciled to a cordial Participation in this righteous and indispensible War."[36] How encouraging that message from John Adams in 1813 must have been. The first citizen of New England believed that the war Madison had avoided for twelve years was now a "righteous and indispensible War." There was still hope for the Union.

NOTES

1. J. C. A. Stagg, *Mr. Madison's War* (Princeton, N.J., 1983), p. 506; Leonard D. White, *The Jeffersonians* (New York, 1951), p. 36; Henry Adams, *History of the United States of America* (9 vols.; New York, 1930), III, 74.

2. Jefferson recounted to Richard Henry Lee, 22 April 1786, his experience at an English dinner party where a Scottish general told Jefferson "that were America to petition parliament to be again received on their former footing, the petition would be very generally rejected. He was serious in this, and I think it was the sentiment of the company, and is the sentiment perhaps of the nation" Julian P. Boyd et al., eds., *The Papers of Thomas Jefferson* (20 vols. to date; Princeton, N.J., 1950—), IX, 396.

3. Militia of Muskingum County, Ohio, to Madison, 30 September 1809, R. A. Rutland et al., eds., *The Papers of James Madison, Presidential Series* (1 vol. to date; Charlottesville, Va., 1984—), I, 392-93.

4. George Hammond to Jefferson, 12 September 1793, *American State*

Papers: Documents, Legislative and Executive, of the Congress of the United States (38 vols.; Washington, 1832-61), *Foreign Relations,* I, 240.

5. George W. Corner, ed., *The Autobiography of Benjamin Rush* (Princeton, N.J., 1948), p. 181; Jefferson to Madison, 28 December 1794, Paul Leicester Ford, ed., *The Writings of Thomas Jefferson* (10 vols.; New York, 1892-99), VI, 519.

6. See Adams, *History of the United States,* II, 345-59.

7. Madison to Rufus King, 30 April 1802, Princeton University Library.

8. James F. Zimmerman, *Impressment of American Seamen* (New York, 1925), p. 260.

9. "A Convention between the United States and Great Britain," *American State Papers, Foreign Relations,* III, 82-83.

10. John Reeves, *History of the Law of Shipping and Navigation* (1792), quoted in Adams, *History of the United States,* II, 323.

11. Quoted in Merrill Peterson, *James Madison: A Biography in His Own Words* (2 vols.; New York, 1974), II, 255.

12. Madison to Monroe, 24 September 1805, Gaillard Hunt, ed., *The Writings of James Madison* (9 vols.; New York, 1900-1910), VII, 190-91

13. Lewis C. Gray, *History of Agriculture in the Southern United States* (2 vols.; New York, 1941), II, 1031, 1039.

14. Harold S. Schultz, *James Madison* (New York, 1970), p. 139.

15. Madison to Jefferson, 14 September 1805, James Madison Papers, Library of Congress.

16. Madison to Monroe (private letter), 20 March 1807, *ibid.*

17. Madison to Monroe, 17 July 1807, quoted in Schultz, *James Madison,* p. 142.

18. Dumas Malone, *Jefferson the President: Second Term, 1805-1809* (Boston, 1974), p. 482.

19. *Ibid.,* p. 483 (italics added). See also the excellent chapter on Jefferson and the Embargo in Burton Spivak, *Jefferson's English Crisis* (Charlottesville, Va., 1979), pp. 198-225.

20. Quoted in Schultz, *James Madison,* p. 114.

21. Madison to William Pinkney, 1 May 1808, James Madison Papers, Library of Congress.

22. Madison to Orchard Cook, n.d., quoted in Spivak, *Jefferson's English Crisis,* p. 210.

23. Madison to Pinkney, 11 February 1809, James Madison Papers, Library of Congress.

24. Curtis P. Nettels, *The Emergence of a National Economy, 1775-1815* (New York, 1962), p. 328.

25. Schultz, *James Madison,* pp. 139-46. Schultz sums up Madison's tenure in the State Department thus: "Madison as Secretary of State was largely occupied with applying ideas of the 1790's to problems of the next decade."

26. "Universal Peace," William T. Hutchinson, et al., eds. *The Papers of James Madison* (14 vols. to date; Chicago and Charlottesville, Va., 1962–), XIV, 207.
27. From the Republican Meeting of Washington County, Maryland, *Madison Papers: Presidential Series*, I, 26, 64.
28. Madison to Pinkney, 17 March 1809, *ibid.*, I, 56.
29. Presidential Proclamation, 19 April 1809, *ibid.*, I, 125-26.
30. Madison to Jefferson, 3 August 1809, *ibid.*, I, 317.
31. Madison to Jefferson, 23 April 1810, Madison Papers, Library of Congress.
32. From Clay's address to the House of Representatives, December 31, 1811, in *The Works of Henry Clay*, ed. Calvin Colton (10 vols.; New York, 1904), I, 187.
33. Samuel Eliot Morison, *By Land and By Sea* (New York, 1953), pp. 266-80.
34. Madison to Jefferson, 3 April 1812, Madison Papers, Library of Congress.
35. Madison to Jefferson, 25 May 1812, *ibid.*
36. Adams to Madison, 14 March 1813, Adams Family Papers, Massachusetts Historical Society.

4

JAMES MONROE AND THE PERSISTENCE OF REPUBLICAN VIRTUE

Harry Ammon

James Monroe, the fifth President and the last revolutionary veteran to hold that office, enjoyed an opportunity denied his predecessors to realize long standing American foreign policy objectives. The termination of the wars following the French Revolution had eliminated the threat to American commerce and security which had dominated foreign policy since the first Washington administration. Moreover, the nation was basking in a sense of self assurance, the result of the conviction that the War of 1812 had won for the United States recognition as an independent power. Monroe was uniquely equipped by his political and diplomatic background to capitalize on this new state of affairs, having served for more than fifteen years in a variety of diplomatic posts, including the secretaryship of state.[1]

Born in Westmoreland County, Virginia, in 1758, Monroe at seventeen enlisted in the Virginia line, winning distinction for bravery at the battle of Trenton. On his return to Virginia he became a close friend and political associate of Thomas Jefferson and James Madison, working with them to strengthen the Confederation and later in the creation of the Republican Party. These early experiences were fundamental in shaping his convictions about the direction the nation should take at home and abroad. Although his approach to foreign policy was molded in terms of the moral imperative of the revolutionary generation and the republican ideals forged during the party conflicts of the 1790s, Monroe never lost sight of the concerns which constituted essential national interests.

It was during his service from 1783 to 1786 in the Confederation Congress as a member of the Virginia delegation that he made a major contribution to the shaping of the new nation's basic foreign policies. His correspondence with Jefferson and Madison demonstrated not only his concern for the problems which Adams and Jefferson faced in Europe but also his conviction that only a greater show of national unity, embodied in congressional control of American commerce, would bring any satisfactory commercial arrangements with the European powers. In December, 1784, he informed Jefferson of his appointment as the first United States minister to France and thereafter he informed Jefferson of developments in America that impinged on external affairs. Upon Benjamin Franklin's return to Philadelphia in 1785 Jefferson warned Monroe to assure a proper reception for the distinguished American citizen and diplomat.

Monroe was responsible for the report which instructed the commissioners to Spain that the *sine qua non* of any treaty with that nation must be the recognition of the thirty-first parallel as the boundary of Florida and an absolute guarantee of the free navigation of the Mississippi River. Understanding that the future development of the West depended upon the right of the United States to keep the river open to American commerce, Monroe was the principal organizer in 1786 of the successful effort to prevent Secretary of Foreign Affairs John Jay from negotiating an agreement with Don Diego de Gardoqui, the Spanish minister, which would have closed the Mississippi for thirty years in return for trade concessions in Spanish ports. Monroe joined Madison in the movement for a new constitution which would at last give the federal government the powers necessary to coerce the European powers into granting American commerce free access to the markets of Europe.

Monroe's next foray into the realm of foreign relations was a less happy one. In 1794, when President Washington dispatched Federalist John Jay to Great Britain, Monroe received an appointment as minister to Revolutionary France to appease Republican critics who feared that Hamilton's policies would produce a rupture with France. Because Monroe interpreted his mission as the sole means of preserving Franco-American amity in the face of what the French considered Washington's pro-British policy, he often behaved more as a party spokesman than as a representative of the United States government. He concluded his address to the National Convention in Paris by expressing the hope that

> by doing everything in my power to preserve and perpetuate the harmony so happily subsisting at present between the two Republics, I shall promote the interest of both. To this great object therefore all my efforts will be directed. If I shall be so fortunate as to succeed in such manner as to merit the approbation of both Republics I shall deem it the happiest event of my life, and return hereafter with a consolation, which those who mean well and have served the cause of liberty alone can feel.

Monroe's ideological assumption that republics should draw close to one another was a direct defiance of Federalist principles as embodied above all in Hamilton's public papers. President Washington's dissatisfaction with Monroe's open friendliness towards the French revolutionary regime led to his abrupt recall. Monroe defended his conduct in a lengthy pamphlet, much admired by his Republican colleagues, which condemned Washington's foreign policy.

Because of Monroe's close identification with Western interests, President Jefferson sent him to France in 1803 as a special envoy to join resident minister Robert R. Livingston in purchasing a port of deposit on the lower Mississippi. Spanish authorities had suspended the right of deposit prior to turning over Louisiana to Napoleon, who had secretly acquired the colony. When Monroe arrived in Paris, Napoleon presented the American envoys with the choice of buying all of Louisiana or nothing. Although not authorized by their instructions to purchase the whole of Louisiana, Monroe and Livingston promptly made that choice, a decision which Jefferson approved despite his doubts regarding the constitutionality of such an extensive territorial acquisition. Popular approval of the purchase established Monroe as a national figure in line for the presidential succession. From 1803 to 1807 (except for an excursus to Madrid in an unsuccessful attempt to obtain Spanish consent to the transfer of Louisiana) Monroe and special envoy William Pinkney, hoping to reduce the tensions between England and America, concluded a treaty with the London government providing for a modification of British commercial restrictions, but without a formal proviso banning impressment. Monroe, who was convinced that the British would never abandon the principle but would cease impressment in practice, accepted an informal pledge to that effect from the British commissioners. However, Jefferson and Secretary of State Madison, considering a formal provision an essential condition, declined to submit the treaty to the Senate for ratification.

In 1811 President Madison named Monroe secretary of state. Monroe entered the cabinet committed to the position that unless the British revoked the Orders-in-Council and abandoned impressment, war was the only alternative for the preservation of national honor. Since there was no clear evidence that Napoleon had modified his system, the British government refused to alter its policy. In spite of the intense pressure Monroe brought to bear on the French Minister, who came to dread his conferences with the secretary of state, he was unable to obtain the proof demanded by the British that Napoleon had in fact modified his commercial restrictions in favor of the United States. Perhaps the most useful service Monroe rendered the President was functioning as a liaison with members of Congress to ensure the adoption of measures necessary to prepare the country for war. When peace commissioners were appointed in 1813, Monroe drafted instructions adhering to the long established administration policy, making the inclusion of a ban on impressment a mandatory condition for the conclusion of peace. In the summer of 1814 Madison, faced by a growing stalemate over this issue in the negotiations at Ghent, reviewed the American position with the cabinet. Responding to Monroe's advice, he authorized new instructions to postpone discussions over impressment until a future date. These new instructions enabled the American commissioners to negotiate the Treaty of Ghent.

During the last six months of the war, Monroe also served as secretary of war. At the end of the struggle, in the midst of the demands on his time for preparing plans for the reduction of the army and his own preoccupation with the coming presidential election, Monroe concluded the negotiations leading to the demilitarization of the Great Lakes (known as the Rush-Bagot Agreement, since Richard Rush was acting secretary of state when it was formally approved in 1817).

Elected to the presidency in 1816 with only token Federalist opposition (183 electoral votes to 34 for Rufus King), Monroe chose as secretary of state John Quincy Adams, the one American whose diplomatic experience was more extensive than the President's. It was not experience alone that led Monroe to turn to Adams. Monroe wanted to include a New Englander in the cabinet, and at the same time disassociate the office of secretary of state from the notion that the incumbent was the hand picked successor to the presidency. Monroe was mistaken in his expectation that a diplomat so long absent would not appear as a likely presidential prospect. Within a few months after his arrival in Washington, Adams was considered a serious contender for the presidency with a substantial Congressional following.

II

The choice of Adams proved a happy one. Not only were they in close agreement about central foreign policy objectives, but also a remarkable working relationship developed between them. They complemented each others' strengths and compensated for their limitations. The President was inclined to be slow in making decisions, reflecting on every aspect of the particular issue. He generally preferred a moderate to an extreme course of action. Adams, on the hand, was quick to draw conclusions, taking strong positions sustained by sharply worded arguments. Monroe lacked Adams' talent as a writer, having a rather turgid prose style without clear focus. Adams' state papers, still admired today, were masterly in their logical exposition and total command of the revelant facts. Monroe was familiar with past foreign policy issues, but he did not have Adams' scholarly grasp of detail. Often impatient at Monroe's slowness, Adams did appreciate the soundness of his judgment. One trait Adams admired, perhaps because he himself lacked it, was the President's willingness to listen to advice—it was, he said, a quality "which in so high a place is an infallible test of a great mind."[2] They differed as much in appearance as in temperament. Monroe was described by a visitor in 1821 "as an old man in black breeches—boots—hair turned up, talks a little thick, motions with his hands when talking—sociable, sedate—about 5 feet 10 or 11 inches tall, rather spare."[3] Adams, ten years younger than his chief, was short, plump, and balding. What he lacked in dignity he possessed in the charm and breadth of his conversation in intimate circles.

In the pages of his diary Adams has left a detailed account not only of his relationship with the President but of the inner working of the administration. Monroe assigned Adams a more significant role in the day to day management of foreign policy than that accorded to any previous secretary of state. All negotiations and all official business with resident diplomats were left entirely in his hands. Monroe limited his contacts with ministers to ceremonial receptions and official social occasions. In making this arrangement Monroe was deliberately reacting against the usages of Jefferson and Madison who had permitted diplomats to approach them directly on official business. In Monroe's opinions this casual behavior had resulted in needless confusion. Monroe defined Adams's role along the lines of the European practice of restricting diplomatic intercourse to the office of the foreign secretary. This shift did not mean that Monroe relinquished control over policy. On the contrary, he not only made all policy decisions, but through regular, at times daily, meetings with Adams he kept himself informed of the details of current negotiations, indicating the direction he wished Adams to pursue in subsequent conferences. He not only read all instructions and state papers composed by Adams, but made frequent alterations. At times he prepared drafts for the use of the secretary. Since Monroe usually stated his wishes precisely, the revisions tended to be in wording and tone—Adams was inclined to be too acerbic on controversial issues for the President's taste. Indeed, once when Monroe returned a document without changes, Adams, who was often irked by revisions, considered the occasion sufficiently noteworthy to merit a comment in his diary.[4]

While Monroe relied primarily on Adams' advice, he also conferred with the cabinet upon major issues. In these meetings discussion ranged freely with opinions frankly expressed. The secretary of war, John C. Calhoun, and the secretary of the treasury, William H. Crawford, were outspoken on foreign policy issues. As befitted rivals for the presidential succession, they were frequently in disagreement. Attorney General William Wirt, who had no political ambitions, said little. The three successive incumbents in the Navy Department, Benjamin Crowningshield, Smith Thompson, and Samuel Southard rarely commented on matters outside their departmental concerns. In consulting the cabinet Monroe was not merely seeking advice but, more importantly, establishing a consensus. Having fostered the elimination of the old party system, Monroe had to rely for support in Congress on the substantial following which Crawford, Calhoun, and Adams could muster among the legislators. The persistence of the caucus system of nomination inevitably made Congress the focus of presidential politics. Thus cabinet backing was essential in counteracting the influence in the House of Henry Clay, the other major presidential aspirant, a frequent critic of administration programs. Monroe never introduced issues in the cabinet on which agreement was impossible. In those instances when opinion was sharply divided, as in the case of Andrew Jackson's conduct during the invasion of Florida in 1818, Monroe usually opted for a middle ground acceptable to all the secretaries.

Monroe's foreign policy adhered to the lines established during the Washington administrations and followed by Jefferson and Madison. He continued the drive for agreements incorporating full commercial reciprocity and recognition of the American position on maritime rights. Territorial expansion, in particular the acquisition of Florida, remained a central objective. As a participant in the Louisiana purchase, Monroe gave high priority to the delineation of the still undefined boundaries of Louisiana. In pursuing these aims Monroe and Adams not only reiterated long familiar arguments but skillfully exploited opportunities arising from international developments. Monroe was sensitive to public opinion as expressed in Congress and the press, but when essential national interests were at stake he provided the leadership necessary to achieve his policy goals. The most innovative aspect of Monroe's policies was his receptiveness to British overtures for the formation of an Anglo-America entente as a counterweight to the European concert of powers. This quest for a closer understanding with the United States was begun at the end of the War of 1812 by the British Foreign Secretary Viscount Robert Castlereagh and continued by his successor, George Canning. Its first fruits had been the Rush-Bagot agreement, demilitarizing the northern frontier, negotiated while Monroe was secretary of state and ratified shortly after he became President. Ultimately the move for rapprochement failed because of British reluctance to make concessions of ancient grievances and domestic political broils over the presidential succession.

III

The most immediate issue confronting Monroe after his inauguration arose from the collapse of Spain's American empire under the pressure of colonial revolutionary forces. Monroe was genuinely sympathetic with the Latin American insurgents, judging these revolutions in terms of his commitment to the ideals of republican government. During the Washington administrations, when Monroe had been minister to France, he had been critical of the President's failure to give public approval to the French revolutionary regime. Monroe did not advocate military action on behalf of France, but only a neutrality which would favor France over Great Britain. Monroe's outspoken enthusiasm for the revolution while in France had led Washington to recall him. Monroe was determined that during his presidency the nation should never again fail in its duty to endorse the cause of republicanism. Although anxious to demonstrate his support for the insurgents, Monroe was concerned that it be done in such a way as not to jeopardize negotiations with Spain for the cession of Florida or provoke European intervention. American pragmatic interests had to be balanced with idealistic aspirations.

Monroe outlined his Latin American policy in 1820 in precise terms in a letter to Albert Gallatin:

> With respect to the Colonies, the object has been to throw into their scale, in a moral sense, the weight of the United States, without so deep a commitment as to make us a party to the contest. All Europe must expect that the citizens of the United States wish success to the Colonies, and all that they can claim, even Spain herself, is that we will maintain an impartial neutrality between the parties. By taking this ground openly and frankly, we acquit ourselves to our own consciences; we accommodate the feelings of our constituents; we render to the Colonies all the aid we can render them, for I am satisfied that had we even joined them in the war, we should have done them more harm than good, as we might have drawn all Europe on them, not to speak of the injury we should have done to ourselves.[5]

The insurgent cause stirred a sympathetic response through the nation. Henry Clay, responding to this enthusiasm, emerged in Congress as an advocate of the immediate recognition of the newly established governments. Monroe, sharing as he did the public enthusiasm, still held back lest premature action provide Spain with justification for rebuffing his efforts to secure Florida. Moreover, Adams, whose influence on this point cannot be disregarded, was not convinced that the insurgent governments were truly republican. He also had doubts about the stability of these regimes. In response to Congressional pressure and public clamor, Monroe late in 1817 sent a three man commission to report on the new governments. Unfortunately for the advocates of recognition the commissioners were in such disagreement that the final report did not present a favorable view of the revolutionary governments.[6] During the next few years Monroe limited himself to general statements in his annual messages expressing approval of the revolutionary movement. In a more pragmatic way he supported the passage of neutrality laws which operated decidedly to the advantage of the insurgents.

As far back as 1804, after returning from an abortive mission to Spain to obtain recognition of the Louisana purchase, Monroe had concluded that Spain would never cede territory in North America except under threat of force.[7] Shortly after he entered office Monroe put his conclusion to the test. In the fall of 1817 he exerted direct pressure on Spain by authorizing an expedition to evict pirates (many claiming to be insurgent privateers) from Amelia Island in the St. Mary's River and hence within Spanish jurisdiction. Not long after, he appointed General Andrew Jackson commander of a punitive expedition to punish those who had been using Florida as a base for frontier raids. Monroe's object was to exact concessions from Spain by advertising that country's inability to maintain order in Florida. When Monroe informed Congress in January, 1818, of the success of the operation against Amelia Island, he made his purpose clear with a direct warning to Spain:

> For these injuries, especially those proceeding from Amelia Island, Spain would be responsible if it was not manifest that . . . she was utterly unable to prevent them. Her territory, however, ought not to be made instrumental, through her inability to defend it, to purposes injurious to the United States. To a country over which she fails to maintain her authority, and which she permits to be converted to the annoyance of her neighbors, her jurisdiction for the time necessarily ceases to exist. The territory of Spain will nevertheless be respected so far as it may be done consistently with the essential interest and safety of the United States.[8]

Confident that his aims could be realized through direct action, Monroe declined a British offer to mediate in the dispute with Spain.[9]

In invading Florida Jackson went far beyond the intent of the administration. Jackson not only occupied the abandoned post of St. Mark's but evicted the Spanish authorities from Pensacola. To top it off, after a hasty court martial, he executed two British traders accused of inciting the Indians. Monroe was confronted with the possibility of major crises with Spain and Britain. He was also faced with a shrill domestic outcry that Jackson had in fact committed an act of war against Spain and thereby had infringed on the power to declare war vested in Congress by the Constitution. When in June, 1818, Monroe received news of Jackson's conduct, he cut short his tour of the Chesapeake fortifications, hastening back to the capital for a series of cabinet meetings as heated as the scorching July temperatures. The debate in the cabinet bluntly exposed the political ambitions of Crawford and Calhoun, who viewed the General's growing fame as a threat to their presidential aspirations. They vehemently urged Monroe to repudiate the General publicly. Adams, reflecting on Spain's impotence and the obvious desire of Castlereagh to avoid controversy with the United States, insisted that Jackson must be fully supported; to repudiate him would be to loose the advantage gained over Spain.[10] After patiently listening to the secretaries, Monroe advanced a solution which would retain the American initiative in negotiations with Spain, appease Jackson's friends, and silence those condemning the General for violating the Constitution. Monroe made his decision public in the annual message of November 16, 1818.[11] Jackson, he informed Congress, had in fact exceeded his instructions, but had done so on information received during the invasion indicating that Spanish officials had encouraged the Indians. Although the administration intended no unfriendliness towards Spain, American forces would remain in Florida until legitimate authority could be established. All this could have been avoided, he noted, had Spain ceded a territory of little value to her over which she could not exercise control. Monroe hammered his point home a month later when he released Adams' instructions of November 28, 1818, to the American Minister in Spain. In this document, praised by Jefferson as a masterly state paper, Adams put forth in strong terms the arguments Monroe had advanced in moderate phrases in his message.[12]

Monroe's policy had the desired effect. Jackson's friends were gratified and Clay's resolutions censuring the General were defeated. More importantly, the Spanish government authorized its minister, Don Luis de Onís, to negotiate a treaty ceding Florida and defining the Lousiana boundary. The cession of Florida was readily arranged, but the settlement of the Lousiana boundary proved more difficult as Onís and Adams battled over every degree of latitude. The southwestern boundary was ultimately fixed at the Sabine River in accordance with views Monroe had held since 1806.[13] A major triumph for the administration was the extension of the boundary westward from the source of the Arkansas River along the 42nd parallel to the Pacific Ocean. The treaty also provided that the United States assume payment of all claims of its citizens against Spain up to a total of $5,000,000, thus resolving another old controversy. Monroe was truly gratified when the Transcontinental Treaty, concluded in February, 1819, was ratified unanimously. It was, he told Richard Rush, a success resulting from the "pressure on Spain" which he had exerted.[14]

Monroe had never considered Texas part of the Lousiana purchase, and consequently no serious attempt had been made to fix the boundary at the Rio Grande. During the two year delay before Spain ratified the transcontinental treaty Clay and other Congressmen criticized the administration for the neglect of Texas. When Jefferson raised the question in May, 1820, Monroe responded that even if it were possible to obtain Texas by exploiting the delay, he would hesitate lest it reopen the antagonisms recently aroused by the bitter debates over the admission of Missouri. If Texas were added to the Union the northern states would be provoked and the Union again placed in jeopardy. "Having secured the Mississippi and all its waters . . . ought we not be satisfied," he asked his old friend, "to take no step which is not approved by all members, or at least a majority of those who accomplished our revolution."[15]

Monroe was so exasperated by Spain's failure to ratify within the six month's stipulated in the treaty that he requested authority in his annual message of 1819 to occupy Florida if ratification were not received within a reasonable length of time. A resolution drafted to this effect was submerged during the furor over the Missouri question. In the late spring of 1820, when Monroe learned that a new Spanish Minister was en route, he asked that the resolution be postponed. Still more delays followed before the treaty was ratified by the new liberal regime in Spain, brought to power in the revolution of 1820. It was with understandable pride that Monroe proclaimed in his second inaugural: "We now . . . comprise within our limits the dimensions and faculties of a great power under a Government possessing all the energies of any government ever known to the Old World, with an utter incapacity to oppress the people."[16]

On March 8, 1822, a year after the ratification of the Transcontinental Treaty, Monroe informed Congress that he was extending formal recognition to Chile, the United Provinces of La Plata (Argentina), Peru and Colombia. He acknowledged that recognition might invite European intervention, but as he told Madison, the "time had certainly arrived when it became our duty to recognize them . . . and not permit them, under a feeling of resentment towards us, and the artful practices of the European powers, to become the dupes of their policy."[17] Working under the President's supervision Adams drew up instructions for the new missions defining American objectives as the encouragement of political, commercial and religious liberty. The ministers were urged to promote the development of an American system different from the monarchical systems of Europe. In the last paragraph of the instructions for Richard C. Anderson, the Minister to Colombia, Monroe's voice can be clearly heard: "The emancipation of the South American Continent opens to the whole race of man prospects of futurity, in which this union will be called in the discharge of its duties to itself and to the unnumbered ages of posterity to take a conspicuous and leading part. It invokes all that is precious in hope . . . to countless millions of our fellow creatures, which in the progressive revolutions of time this hemisphere is destined to rear and maintain."[18]

IV

Monroe's success in the Spanish negotiations was not matched in other areas which he considered equally important. In spite of persistent efforts, he was unable to obtain from either France or Great Britain trade treaties on a basis of full reciprocity — a principle alien to their historic commercial policies. At the end of the War of 1812 the American commissioners in London had been obliged to accept an agreement providing for reciprocity only between American ports and those of the United Kingdom in Europe. West Indian ports, the focus of a trade considered vital to American interests, were excluded. In 1818 Monroe was sufficiently encouraged by Viscount Castlereagh's friendly attitude to hope for an agreement based on full reciprocity in all ports. It also seemed an opportune moment to resolve long standing disagreements over the fisheries, boundaries, and compensation for slaves removed by British forces at the end of the war. The instructions Adams penned for Richard Rush, the Minister in London, omitted one ancient quarrel. The issue of impressment was not to be raised unless the British indicated a willingness to negotiate. Monroe undoubtedly assumed that there was little point in raising this question, since the British government had shown no interest in a proposal he made as secretary of state and renewed through Rush in 1817. At that time Monroe had suggested that impressment be banned on the condition that neither party permit naturalized citizens to serve in their respective navies or merchant marines.

Albert Gallatin, the American Minister to France, was dispatched to London to join the relatively inexperienced Rush. Finding the British inflexibly committed to the old colonial system, they had no choice but to renew the trade agreement of 1815 for a ten year period. However, on other issues Castlereagh made significant concessions. Although Adams, faithful to his father's stance on the fisheries, had argued that the American claim should be defended as a right, Monroe overruled him, approving an agreement granting extensive privileges "for ever" without defining the basis of the claim. Equally important was an agreement to fix the northwest boundary along the forty-ninth parallel from the Lake of the Woods to the Rocky Mountains. The disposition of Oregon was left to future negotiations. Castlereagh also agreed that the question of an indemnity for slaves should be referred to arbitration. In 1826 the United States was awarded $1,200,000 to satisfy the claimants.

Surprisingly, Castlereagh was willing to approve a ban on impressment along the lines previously suggested by Monroe but with two modifications: first, that the United States supply a list of naturalized citizens, and, second, that the treaty be limited to ten years subject to six months cancellation by either party. Unfortunately Castlereagh departed for the Congress of Aix-la-Chapelle just as British negotiators began discussing this touchy question. Both parties soon bogged down in haggling over minor details. In the absence of clear-cut instructions, Rush and Gallatin declined incorporating provisions on impressment in the final convention which they signed on October 20, 1818. Across the Atlantic just ten days later, Monroe reviewed the British proposal with the cabinet. He was inclined to accept the arrangement, if the cancellation period were made longer than six months. The British, he noted, had never made such extensive concessions. Adams and Calhoun were strongly opposed to an agreement permitting the British to muster crews on American vessels (even if restricted to British waters) in order to check the roster against a list of naturalized citizens. They could not approve a departure from the American position on maritime rights. Concerned that the Senate might not ratify a convention including these provisions, Monroe decided not to instruct the American commissioners to incorporate them.[19] Not until 1823 did Monroe raise the issue again. The limited commercial provisions incorporated in the convention were a major disappointment. As a retaliatory measure Monroe supported bills (collectively known as the Navigation Acts) which effectively excluded from American ports British ships clearing from the West Indies.[20]

At the beginning of Monroe's administration France's commercial policy was as unfavorable to American trade as that of Great Britain. The restoration government had imposed discriminatory tariffs and tonnage duties on American shipping. In 1820, after repeated efforts to secure modification of these duties, Monroe, acting on Gallatin's advice, obtained the enactment of a bill imposing retaliatory charges. When France replied in kind, the direct trade between the two countries declined drastically. Commercial negotiations with France were complicated by controversies over spoliation claims dating from the Napoleonic era, the status of French ships in Lousiana ports, and protests over the seizure of several French ships charged with smuggling. In the fall of 1821 discussions between Adams and the usually amiable French Minister, Hyde de Neuville, were so acrimonious that Monroe contemplated requesting his recall. Adams suggested instead that the President review the controversy in his annual message, leaving the door open to continued negotiation. The moderate language used in his message of December 3, 1821, achieved the intended results. The French government now presented a compromise proposing that discriminatory duties be mutually reduced by one-fourth annually until eliminated or the agreement cancelled by either party. Adams considered the offer inadequate, but Monroe approved the arrangement. This the Senate ratified with only three dissenting votes. The other issues with France remained unsettled during Monroe's tenure.[21]

Midway in his second term Monroe renewed the earlier attempt to settle the long standing controversies with Great Britain. The new Foreign Secretary, George Canning, had continued the friendly overtures initiated by Castlereagh. The time seemed propitious in view of the growing detachment of Great Britain from the concert of Europe. Moreover, shifts in American opinion had opened the way for the administration to modify its rigid position on maritime rights on at least one issue and thus facilitate an Anglo-American rapprochement. The two nations also had common interests in

Latin America and on the Pacific northwest coast. In 1822 protests lodged separately by the United States and Great Britain had obtained a suspension of the Tsar's ukase asserting Russian control of the Pacific coast to the 51st parallel. Might not the two powers now jointly negotiate with Russia? Consequently, in the summer of 1823 Adams drew up nine sets of instructions for Rush which were carefully revised by the President. They ranged over commercial reciprocity, impressment, the status of consuls, and the Oregon question. With one exception, they did not raise any new issues. In the instructions (No. 65, June 24, 1823) accompanying a draft convention one new topic appeared—the suppression of the slave trade.

Before Rush could broach the issues raised in his instructions, Canning made a proposal so startling that Rush promptly referred the matter to Washington. Canning suggested that the United States and Great Britain jointly declare their opposition to any project by the European powers to restore Spain's colonies. He also wished the declaration to include a statement affirming that neither party intended to acquire any of Spain's possessions. Canning's offer was prompted by France's active interest in intervening on Spain's behalf. Unable to prevent France from invading Spain in 1823 to suppress the liberal regime, Canning was determined to prevent an intrusion into the Americas, where British merchants had developed a significant trade. In shaping policy towards the insurgents Canning, unlike Monroe, was not moved by sympathy for republican institutions but solely by the need to protect British commercial interests.

When he received Rush's dispatch in October, 1823, Monroe promptly consulted Jefferson and Madison, who urged acceptance. Canning's offer was unexpected, but the idea of Anglo-American cooperation in Latin America was not a novel one to Monroe. During his ministry to Great Britain Monroe had been impressed by the pro-republican sympathies expressed by the English Whigs in contrast to the hostility manifested by the Tories. He had been on intimate terms with Lord Holland, the nephew of the Whig leader Charles Fox. At that time Monroe had discussed with Lord Holland the possibility of a joint policy towards the Spanish colonies in which rebellions had commenced.[22] Canning's proposal was tempting, but Monroe did not trust him. It was not just that Canning was a Tory with a reputation for duplicity, but his predecessor had not responded to Monroe's suggestion in 1818 that Britain move to recognize the independence of the former Spanish colonies. To join Canning, known to be ill-disposed towards republican institutions, would seem to place the United States in league with monarchical forces.

In presenting Canning's proposal to the cabinet Monroe did not mention the advice given by Jefferson and Madison; nor did he indicate his preference. All the secretaries participated except Crawford, who was ill, but only Calhoun and Adams offered extensive comments. Monroe was tempted by an offer which would place the United States on an equal footing with the European powers, but he did not want the nation to appear in a secondary position to Great Britain. Calhoun, genuinely convinced that armed intervention was imminent, urged Monroe to accept the British proposal, perhaps even giving Rush discretionary power. Adams, responding to Monroe's apprehension that the allied powers were about to mount an invasion—after all Canning had presented the threat as real—persuasively argued that the British fleet alone was sufficient to prevent a French expedition if one were undertaken. Adams also pointed out, and on this there was agreement, that Canning's proposal might well be a screen to exact a pledge from the United States not to annex Cuba, an acquisition many American thought imminent. Adams also stressed, and on this point Monroe concurred, that the people would not approve such a close bond with the nation's ancient enemy. In mid-November, following Monroe's instructions, Adams began to draft a letter to Rush authorizing him to inform Canning that the United States was not prepared to act jointly, although it approved the principles outlined by the Foreign Minister. In the event of an emergency making "a joint manifestations of opinion" desirable Rush was to refer the question to the President.[23] By the time Adams began to prepare these instructions, dispatches from Rush indicated that the threat of intervention had apparently receded; Canning no longer seemed interested in joint action. What Rush did not know was that Canning had obtained from the French government a statement (known as the Polignac Memorandum) denying any intention to act against the Spanish colonies by force of arms. Not until late December did Canning inform Rush of this agreement.

The method of replying to Canning via Rush had one disadvantage—the American position would not be publicly known, since the foreign secretary's communication had been made informally. To ensure publicity for the administration's position Monroe decided to incorporate a statement condemning European intervention in American affairs in a response to a note submitted by the Russian minister. In this note the minister had transmitted a circular letter of the Russian foreign secretary expressing the Tsar's gratification at the success of the allies in protecting Europe from the perils of revolution. While Adams worked on the reply to the Russian minister, Monroe began to draft his annual message. Following his usual practice, he requested the secretaries to submit paragraphs on matters concerning their departments. As he received and revised these contributions, he read sections of the message to the cabinet. At an early stage he included verbatim a passage drawn up by Adams declaring that the "American continents by the free and independent conditions which they have assumed, and maintain, are henceforth not to be considered as a subject for future colonization by any European power."[24] It was in this manner that a basic principle of the message of December 2, 1823, was formulated. It was exclusively the contribution of Adams, who was more concerned about Russian expansion on the Northwest coast than a putative invasion of South America.

On November 21 Monroe startled the department heads, as he read paragraphs strongly condemning the recent actions of the allied powers in Europe. He also recommended that Congress appropriate funds to send a minister to Greece. Adams was so perturbed by Monroe's provocative remarks about the allied powers and by what he deemed premature action on Greece that he privately interceded with the president to modify his remarks. Adams preferred that the United States take its stand against European interference in South America while it disclaimed any American intent to interfere with Europe.[25] A few days later, when Monroe again read portions of his message, the reference to Greek recognition had vanished to be replaced by a warm endorsement of the Greek revolution, then a popular cause. The condemnation of the allied powers was substantially softened. It was at this meeting that he read the paragraphs on Latin America which constitute, along with Adams' non-colonization principle, the Monroe Doctrine, as the President's statement came to be labelled.

Monroe's message covered a variety of topics with the larger portion devoted to domestic affairs. Early in the message, after reviewing relations with Russia, he enunciated the non-colonization principle. Not until the final paragraphs did he refer to the policies of the allied powers. After observing that the political system of the European states was essentially different from that of the United States, the President continued:

> We owe it, therefore, to candor and to the amicable
> relations existing between the United States and those
> powers to declare that we should consider any attempt
> on their part to extend their system to any portion of
> this hemisphere as dangerous to our peace and safety. . . .
> But with those governments who have declared their
> independence . . . we could not view any interposition
> . . . by any European power in any other light than as
> the manifestation of an unfriendly disposition toward
> the United States. . . . [26]

As a third element in his famed doctrine Monroe reaffirmed the American policy of non-interference in the internal affairs of other nations.[27]

Monroe's message was enthusiastically greeted at home and favorably commented upon in the British press. Even that perennial critic, Henry Clay, not only praised it but indicated his willingness, if the President desired, to sponsor supportive resolutions in the House. Canning was not pleased by what he considered an American attempt to win the credit for checking the European powers. Unquestionably Monroe's message put a chill on the move for better Anglo-American understanding. To ensure that his government received recognition as the protector of Latin American independence Canning released the Polignac Memorandum in the spring of 1824. At the time Monroe's declaration was not considered extraordinarily important. Contemporary Americans interpreted it as no more than a reiteration of the general conviction that there existed an American system radically different from the institutions of the old world.

V

Monroe and Adams had once hoped that Britain would join the United States in negotiating with Russia over the Northwest coast. However, Canning's distaste for the non-colonization principle was such that he declined to participate. Monroe's pronouncement, however, did not impede American negotiations in St. Petersburg. Count Nesselrode, the Russian foreign minister, proposed to the American minister, Henry Middleton, that the discussions be restricted solely to issues of mutual interest. On this basis Middleton concluded an agreement in April, 1824, fixing 54′40″ as the dividing line between their respective spheres of activity. Monroe was especially pleased by this manifestation of friendship so much in contrast to British attitudes. The following year the British government negotiated an agreement with Russia along similar lines.[28]

When Rush approached Canning about the issues outlined in the instructions drawn up in the summer of 1823, Canning expressed interest in only one item — the suppression of the slave trade. Since the end of the war, first Castlereagh and then Canning had sought to persuade the United States and the European powers to create an international patrol to eradicate the slave trade. Spain, Portugal, and the Netherlands had already subscribed, accepting the fact that enforcement would of necessity be dependent on British sea power. In 1818 Monroe, strongly supported by Adams and Calhoun, had rejected British overtures because he was unwilling to grant even a limited right of search on the high seas. In the next few years lobbying by the American Colonization Society produced a shift in Congressional opinion. Early in 1823 the House adopted, by a majority of 139 to 9, a resolution recommending that the President negotiate with the European powers to condemn the slave trade as piracy. An agreement on this basis would by-pass the issue of maritime rights, since pirates could not claim the protection of any national flag. Monroe welcomed this opening. He was a slave owner, but his hostility towards the institution and his hope of its eventual elimination were well known. If the slave trade were defined as piracy, there could be no objection to permitting an international patrol to stop and search American ships on the high seas.

Adams was by no means happy over the President's decision to negotiate along the lines of the congressional resolution. When Monroe informed the cabinet of his intention to negotiate on the basis, both Adams and Calhoun spoke out opposing any departure from existing policy on maritime rights. Adams, obviously concerned about the approaching presidential election, believed that he would be blamed for yielding a basic American right. The fact that Crawford, the leading rival for the presidency, was ardently advocating the negotiation, led him to suspect that his colleague was deliberately plotting to discredit him. Nonetheless, Adams, as ever loyal to his chief, drafted instructions and drew up a treaty project in conformity with the wishes of the President. Monroe, who was always sensitive to the feelings of his secretaries, permitted Adams to include in the instructions to Rush a defense of the American position of maritime rights.

93

Canning promptly accepted the agreement, securing from Parliament a condemnation of the slave trade as piracy. In view of the overwhelming vote in the House, Monroe anticipated prompt ratification. To his dismay objections were raised about permitting foreign ships to stop and search American vessels on the high seas. Adams quite correctly concluded that the attack on the treaty was mounted primarily to embarrass him. The opposition was directed by Senator Martin Van Buren, the organizer of Crawford's campaign. When Monroe appealed to Crawford to rally his friends in behalf of the convention, the secretary of the treasury, who was still seriously ill, not only declined to intervene but also denied that he had ever approved the proposal. Since Van Buren was unable to muster the votes needed to block ratification, he concentrated his efforts on an amendment which limited the right of search to African coastal waters, a restriction which would render the agreement ineffective. Anxious to secure ratification without changes in a treaty which the United States had proposed, Monroe resorted in May, 1824, to the then unusual expedient of sending a special message. He argued that the convention sacrificed no basic American right. "It cannot be disguised," he added, "that the rejection of this convention cannot fail to have a very injurious influence on the good understanding between the two governments. . . . " His plea was in vain. The Senate ratified with the restrictive amendment. Canning, exasperated by the change, refused to accept the amended text and suspended negotiations with Rush on the other issues Adams had raised in his instructions of 1823. The hopes for a rapprochement faded as the conflict over the presidential succession preempted all other issues. It was not a happy close to a diplomatic era in which the successes had far outnumbered the failures.[29]

NOTES

1. In preparing this essay I have drawn heavily upon the many scholarly studies of Monroe's foreign policy. The most important are: Samuel Falgg Bemis, *John Quincy Adams and the Foundations of American Foreign Policy* (New York, 1949); Bradford Perkins, *Castlereagh and Adams: England and the United States, 1812–1823* (Berkeley, CA, 1964); Harry Ammon, *James Monroe, The Quest for National Identity* (New York, 1971); Dexter Perkins, *The Monroe Doctrine, 1823–1826.* In *Harvard Historical Studies,* vol. XXXIX (Cambridge, Mass., 1927); Arthur P. Whitaker, *The United States*

and the Independence of Latin America (Baltimore, 1941); Philip Colidge Brooks, *Diplomacy and the Borderlands: The Adams-Onis Treaty of 1819.* In *University of California Historical Publications,* XXIV (1939); Hugh B. Soulsby, *The Right of Search and the Slave Trade in Anglo-American Relations, 1814-1862* (Baltimore, 1931); Robert A. McLemore, *Franco-American Diplomatic Relations, 1816-1836* (Baton Rouge, 1941); F. Lee Benns, *The American Struggle for the British West Indian Carrying Trade, 1815-1830.* In Indiana University Studies, X, no. 56. From the British point of view: C. K. Webster, *The Foreign Policy of Castlereagh* (2 vols., London, 1931); Harold Temperley, *The Foreign Policy of Canning, 1822-1827* (London, 1925).

2. John Quincy Adams, *Memoirs.* ed., by Charles Frances *Adams* (12 vols., Philadelphia, 1874-77), IV, 470, Dec. 6, 1819.

3. "Extracts from the Diary of William D. Williamson of Bangor, Maine," Dec. 17, 1821, in *New England Historical and Geneological Register,* XXX (1876), p. 429.

4. Adams, *Memoirs,* IV, 16-22, Nov. 7-23, 1817.

5. May 26, 1820. In James Monroe, *Writings.* Ed. by Stanislaus Murray Hamilton (7 vols., New York, 1898-1903), VI, 132.

6. Adams, *Memoirs,* IV, 156-64, Nov. 2-6, 1818.

7. Monroe to Madison, Jan. 9, 1804, Monroe, *Writings,* IV, 123.

8. Special message of Jan. 13, 1818, James Daniel Richardson, ed., *Messages and Papers of the Presidents, 1789-1907* (Washington, 11 vols., 1875-1893), II, 24.

9. Adams, *Memoirs,* IV, 48-51, Jan. 27-31, 1818.

10. *Ibid.,* IV, 114-119, July 15-20, 1818.

11. Richardson, ed., *Messages,* II, 41-43, Nov. 16, 1818.

12. Bemis, *Adams, Foundations,* pp. 321-27.

13. The boundary provisions of the treaty as summarized by Bemis, *Adams, Foundations,* p. 355: The boundary "began at the mouth of the Sabine River in the sea and continued north along the western bank of that river to the 32rd parallel of latitude, thence by a line due north to the Red River, thence westward up the south bank of the Red River to 100° west longitude, thence across the said Red River and due north to the south bank of the Arkansas and westward along that bank to the source in latitude 42° north, and thence westward by that parallel to the South Sea, the whole as laid down in Melish's map."

14. March 7, 1819, Monroe, *Writings,* VI, 91.

15. May 20, 1820, *Ibid.,* VI, 119-23.

16. Richardson, ed., *Messages,* II, 94, Mar. 5, 1821.

17. May 10, 1822, Monroe *Writings,* IV, 285.

18. May 27, 1823, cited in Bemis, *Adams, Foundations,* p. 361.

19. Adams, Memoirs, IV, 146-150, Oct. 29-30, 1818: Bradford Perkins, *Castlereagh and Adams,* pp. 268-73.

20. Benns, *West Indian Carrying Trade,* pp. 68-98.
21. Bemis, *Adams, Foundations,* pp. 450-457.
22. Lady Elizabeth Holland, *Journal 1791-1811* (2 vols., London, 1909), II, 202, 209, Feb. 12, Mar. 2, 1807.
23. Nov. 29, 1839, Monroe, *Writings,* VI, 405-408.
24. Ammon, *Monroe,* p. 481.
25. Adams, *Memoirs,* VI, p. 197, Nov. 22, 1823.
26. Pertinent passages are conveniently quoted in Bemis, *Adams, Foundations,* pp. 391-393.
27. For detailed accounts of the Monroe Doctrine See *Ibid.,* pp. 382-408; Dexter Perkins, *Monroe Doctrine,* and Ammon, *Monroe,* pp. 476-492.
28. Bemis, *Adams, Foundations,* pp. 523-25.
29. *Ibid.,* 409-35; Richardson, *Messages,* II, 243-47, May 21, 1824.

5

JOHN QUINCY ADAMS AND THE FEDERALIST TRADITION

Norman A. Graebner

Historians have judged John Quincy Adams the most accomplished diplomatist in this country's history. Such distinguished performance cannot be divorced from solid intellectual formulations of policy. That Adams possessed remarkable qualities of mind was evident long before 1817. His unique perceptions of international affairs first emerged when he defended President George Washington's Neutrality Proclamation in April and May, 1793. His "Marcellus" papers, which preceded by two months the appearance of Hamilton's noted "Pacificus," revealed at the outset those fundamentals which would guide Adams' thought and action throughout his diplomatic career. His rejection of the plea that the United States support France, then locked in war with Britain, dwelt on the importance of interest and power, not good intentions, in the conduct of foreign relations.

This nation, Adams reminded his readers, had treaties of peace with France, England, Holland, and Prussia, and was not constituted a judge of the respective merits of their causes. "As men," he wrote, "we must undoubtedly lament the effusion of human blood, and the mass of misery and distress which is preparing for the great part of the civilized world; but as the citizens of a nation at a vast distance from the continent of Europe; of a nation whose happiness consists of a real independence, disconnected from all European interests and European politics, it is our duty to remain, the peaceable and silent, though sorrowful spectators of the san-

97

guinary scene." Neutrality, believed Adams, would serve the interests of American commerce; partisanship would serve no countering purpose. Had the king of France remained on his throne and inaugurated the existing war against Europe, the French treaty of alliance—the legal and moral foundation of the pro-French arguments leveled at the Washington administration—could impose no obligation on the United States. No treaty, argued Adams, "can ever oblige one nation to adopt or support the folly or injustice of another." How could the United States aid the French cause when France had declared war on all the naval powers of Europe? To rush to the French cause would submit the country to needless destruction and ruin.[1]

Adams' able defense of Washington's controversial policies propelled him into long periods of service abroad. Washington assigned him to the Netherlands in 1794; his father, as President, kept him in Berlin from 1797 to 1801. Shortly after his return to the United States, Adams entered the United States Senate and there defended the troubled foreign policies of Thomas Jefferson and James Madison against the assaults of the New England Federalists, his erstwhile allies. In 1809 Madison appointed him minister to St. Petersburg. Whatever the contribution of Adams' diplomatic experience in Europe to his capacity as secretary of state, Adams himself was not greatly impressed by his early achievements.[2]

In many external characteristics Adams scarcely resembled the classical diplomatist—suave, even-tempered, reassuring. He was short and bald, with a belligerent demeanor and a rheumy affliction which caused his eyes to run incessantly. But if Adams at times antagonized his associates, he was scarcely more charitable toward himself. Following a dinner at the home of the president of the Bank of the United States in October, 1818, Adams confided to his diary: "I am not satisfied with myself this day, having talked too much at dinner. . . . Yet, in the estimation of others, I pass off on the whole better when I talk freely than when silent and reserved. This sometimes stimulates me to talk more than is wise or proper. . . . Nor can I always (I did not this day) altogether avoid a dogmatical and peremptory tone and manner, always disgusting, and especially offensive in persons to whose age or situation others consider some deference due."[3] On occasion Adams' diary notes were even more pitiless: "I am a man of reserved, cold, austere, and forbidding manners; my political adversaries say, a gloomy misanthropist, and my personal enemies, an unsocial savage. With a knowledge of the actual defect in my character, I have not the pliability to reform it."[4]

Beyond his dogged convictions which neither time nor circumstance would alter, Adams possessed every other quality essential for diplomatic distinction. His understanding of Europe and its relationship to the New World was profound. He understood with equal precision the limits of effective American diplomacy. For Adams no less than for Washington and Hamilton, United States foreign policy had one major purpose: to serve the interests of this country, defined in commercial and geographical terms. He recognized, as had Hamilton in *The Federalist,* the natural separation of the New World from the Old and the essential advantages which the United States enjoyed in its world relationships. Throughout his career Adams denied that a genuine foreign policy could pursue abstract objectives. If he favored liberty, he refused to anchor the nation's foreign policies to its achievement. The means of enforcement, he knew, were not within his control; nor could such an objective be the subject of fruitful negotiations. Thus European diplomats always found Adams direct, reliable, and realistic. Even when he doggedly refused to surrender any advantage, diplomats found him simple-mannered and courteous.

Adams' residence in St. Petersburg during the closing years of the Napoleonic wars made him a natural choice to represent the United States in the negotiations with Britain at Ghent following the War of 1812. With the establishment of peace in 1815, Madison transferred him to London where, like his father in 1785, he assumed the task of negotiating issues left unresolved by war.

II

In 1817 the third member of the Virginia dynasty, James Monroe, invited Adams to enter his cabinet as secretary of state. John Adams advised his son to accept. "You are now approaching fifty years of age," he wrote. "In my opinion you must return to [your country], or renounce it forever. I am well aware of the critical situation you will be in. I know you have not the ... immutable taciturnity of Franklin and Washington. But you must risque all."[5] Jefferson lauded Monroe's choice. "They were made for each other," ran his comment. "Adams has a pointed pen; Monroe has judgment enough for both and firmness enough to have *his* judgment control."[6] Jefferson's was a Republican view, recognizing differences in personality, not philosophy. Monroe and Adams had occupied opposite poles during the great debates of the Washington years. And Adams' earlier convictions were as firm as ever. "The President, I am sure," he wrote to his mother, "will neither require nor expect from me any sacrifice of principles inconsistent with my sense of right."[7] That the two men functioned as an effective team measured not only the overwhelming conversion of the Republicans in power to the older Federalist notions of proper diplomatic behavior, but also Adams' acceptance of his subordinate role in policy-making.[8]

Adams managed the technical aspects of diplomacy with remarkable skill. His diligence compelled him to read all dispatches sent out and received by the State Department. Monroe, equally experienced in foreign affairs, maintained a close surveillance over Adams' correspondence. When, on occasion, Adams objected to Monroe's presidential statements or accepted them only after futile argument, it was because the President had again reacted to events abroad from the standard of simple Republican virtue rather than from a clear recognition of the interests and genuine intentions of the United States. Ultimately it was Adams and not Monroe who gave leadership and direction to American foreign relations during the eight years of their close association.

Adams worked independently, often as a minority of one. He alone among the nation's leaders knew Europe's leading statesmen personally, especially Tsar Alexander, Talleyrand, and Castlereagh. Whatever Adams' convictions that his perceptions were keener than those of his less experienced cabinet colleagues, members of Monroe's powerful cabinet opposed Adams on numerous occasions. Recognizing both the secretary's independence of mind and his refusal to accept views regarded rash by the diplomatic corps, Hyde de Neuville, the French minister, wrote of Adams in December, 1817: "I know that he has dared to declare himself very strongly on many occasions against indiscreet and purely speculative ideas."[9]

For Adams partisanship was as dangerous as it was inexcusable. Earlier he had lamented the Jeffersonian attacks on Washington's foreign policies as well as the opposition of the New England Federalists, his erstwhile allies, to Jefferson and Madison. Of all the wartime deformities in need of elimination, the most disgusting, wrote Adams, "is the rancorous spirit of faction which drove one part of the country headlong towards the dissolution of the union, and towards a treacherous and servile adherence to the enemies of the country. . . . [I]t required little less than a special interposition of Providence to save us from utter disgrace and dismemberment. . . . "[10] For Adams unrestrained partisanship was rooted in politics and personal ambition; to his critics, therefore, he would seldom attribute sincerity.

Adams believed that his judgments should be measured by recognized standards of propriety, their accuracy in reflecting world conditions, and their possible contribution to the country's welfare. Thus he rebuked his critics of the press far more savagely than he did those diplomats who sometimes appeared unnecessarily obdurate. He complained of editors generally on one occasion: "There is not one of them whose friendship is worth buying, nor one whose enmity is not formidable. They are a sort of assassins who sit with loaded blunderbusses at the corner of streets and fire them off for hire or for sport at any passenger whom they select."[11] More pointedly Adams passed judgment in his diary on the editors of the *Aurora* and the *Democratic Press*, both of Philadelphia: "They are both men of considerable talents and profligate principles, always for sale to the highest bidder, and always insupportable burdens, by their insatiable rapacity, to the parties they support."[12]

If Adams, as secretary, faced opposition in the cabinet, the Congress, and the press, he towered over the Washington diplomatic corps. Those compelled to negotiate with him never ceased to admire his intelligence and learning, his industry and self-discipline, his unwavering pursuit of his country's interests, grasped more surely by him than by any other man of his age. Adversaries questioned only his doggedness and disposition. British Minister Stratford Canning wrote of Adams in his memoirs: "He was . . . much above par in general ability, but having the air of a scholar rather than statesman, a very uneven temper, a disposition at times well-meaning, a manner somewhat too often domineering. . . . "[13]

Behind the respect which Adams enjoyed was the essential honesty of his policies. For him the path of virtue was not always clear, nor was virtue always crowned with success. But he believed that a policy, otherwise sound, would be wiser and more enduring if it possessed the quality of virtue. Perhaps there were occasions, especially in time of war, when deception was justifiable; but fraud, believed Adams, was never justifiable where force would not be equally justified. Fraud must be used sparingly, he warned, for "every instance of it . . . tends when discovered to impair the confidence of mankind in the sincerity and integrity of him who uses it."[14] Adams preferred that his country's policies be just, whether successful or not. Stephen Decatur had offered his famous toast: "Our country! In her intercourse with foreign nations, may she always be in the right; but our country, right or wrong." Adams disagreed, writing to his father in August, 1816: "I cannot ask of heaven success, even for my country, in a cause where she should be in the wrong. . . . I disclaim as unsound all patriotism incompatible with the principles of eternal justice. But the truth is that the American union, while united, may be certain of success in every rightful cause, and may if it pleases never have any but a rightful cause to maintain."[15]

From the beginning Adams recognized the limits of American power and influence in Europe. Toward the continent, emerging from a quarter century of war, he urged a posture of strict neutrality. Europe, he wrote in 1815, "consists only of victors and vanquished, between whom no permanent state of social repose can exist. May we persevere in the system of keeping aloof from all their broils, and in that of consolidating and perpetuating our own union."[16] In his noted oration of July 4, 1821, Adams insisted that the United States had conducted its foreign relations in a spirit of friendliness and reciprocity; it had recognized the independence of other countries and maintained its own. America sympathized for the cause of liberty everywhere. "Wherever the standard of freedom and Independence has been or shall be unfurled," he said, "there will her heart, her benedictions and her prayers be. But she goes not abroad, in search of monsters to destroy. She is the well-wisher to the freedom and independence of all. She is the champion and vindicator only of her own. She will comment the general cause by . . . the benignant sympathy of her example."[17] Any shift from liberty to force, Adams warned, might make the United States dictatress of the world and no longer the ruler of its own spirit. To his principle of neutrality Adams added that of non-intervention.

Toward the North American continent Adams was an expansionist, but his expansionism looked to geography, not to war. For him the continent seemed destined to be one nation in language, religion, society, and politics. During November, 1819, secretary of the treasury William H. Crawford informed him that many British and French citizens regarded the United States ambitious and encroaching. Adams replied that to argue otherwise would be useless.

> Nothing that we could say or do [Adams predicted] would remove this impression until the world shall be familiarized with the idea of considering our proper dominion to be the continent of North America. From the time when we became an independent people it was

as much a law of nature that this should become our pretension as that the Mississippi should flow to the sea. Spain had possessions upon our southern and Great Britain upon our northern border. It was impossible that centuries should elapse without finding them annexed to the United States; not that any spirit of encroachment or ambition on our part renders it necessary, but because it is a physical, moral, and political absurdity that such fragments of territory, with sovereigns at fifteen hundred miles beyond sea, worthless and burdensome to their owners, should exist permanently contiguous to a great, powerful, enterprising, and rapidly growing nation. . . . [U]ntil Europe shall find it a settled geographical element that the United States and North American are identical, any effort on our part to reason the world out of a belief that we are ambitious will have no other effect than to convince them that we add to our ambition hypocrisy.[18]

A year later Adams, in conversation with Stratford Canning over the future of Oregon, declared that the London government had certainly come "to the conclusion that there would be neither policy nor profit in cavilling with us about territory on this North American continent." When Canning asked if the secretary included Canada in his claims, Adams responded, "No, there the boundary is marked, and we have no disposition to encroach upon it. Keep what is yours, but leave the rest of the continent to us."[19]

To underwrite his hopes for peace and security in a still challenging world, Adams looked to a stronger union, based on centralized government, and to a reasonable level of military preparedness. "No nation can enjoy freedom and independence," he wrote, "without being always prepared to defend them by force of arms." He reminded Monroe in November, 1814, "We shall have no valuable friends in Europe until we have proved that we can defend ourselves without them."[20] But adequate power—which Adams doubted the country would ever create except in time of war—dared not encourage a mood of belligerency. He advised the country to employ every means available to settle disputes amicably, and never to enter a war "without a fair prospect of attaining its objects." Nor should it remain in a war unless the gains were clearly commensurate with the costs.[21] Such principles and purposes guided Adams in every diplomatic confrontation of his secretarial years.

III

European statesmen recognized the importance of France to the restoration of the balance of power in Europe. As the Declaration of Frankfurt expressed it, the allies desired a great and powerful France "because French power . . . [was] one of the essential foundations of the social structure" of the continent.[22] The restoration of the Bourbons, even the British agreed, would serve the best interests of all nations in a stable Europe. Despite the later condemnation leveled at the Congress of Vienna for its free assignment of territory, the decisions of that notable international conference rather completely underwrote the principle of balance. The Quadruple Alliance which followed in November, 1815, represented the effort of Europe's leading statesmen to carry into peacetime the equilibrium created by the coalition against Napoleon. The later conferences at Troppau (1820), Laibach (1821), and Verona (1822), which adopted interventionist policies toward Italy, Spain, and Portugal, split the great powers. British leaders could detect no threat in liberal uprisings to the allied purpose of maintaining Europe's essential equilibrium. Castlereagh, Britain's greatest foreign minister, broke down in 1822 over his failure to nullify Europe's reactionary policies and took his own life. George Canning, his brilliant successor, withdrew British participation from the affairs of the Quadruple Alliance.[23]

Adams recognized the fundamental purpose of Europe's postwar state system — to prevent the rise again of preponderant power and to restrain threats to the region's stability. But with time Adams also became critical of the Tsar's Holy Alliance and its role in defending the postwar principle of legitimacy. Europe, he complained in April, 1816, had cast off Napoleon only to return to Divine Right.[24] Still through subsequent years the league appeared successful, at least in Europe; in Latin America the challenge to the *status quo* seemed too distant for the European powers to control. Adams saw clearly that the dangers to Europe's stability were internal, that tensions which endangered the peace were between peoples and their rulers. To him it was clear why Russia's Alexander was the principal patron of the European system: "His territories are the most extensive, his military establishment the most stupendous, his country the most improvable and thriving of them all. . . . [H]is circumstances point his policy to a faithful adherence to the general system, with a strong reprobation of those who would resort to special and partial alliances, from which any one member of the league should be excluded."

If Europe's great powers desisted, because of predictable costs, from imposing on one another, they scarcely seemed capable of imposing on the New World. Europe's balance served the American interest in achieving a stable and independent hemisphere, but it did not necessarily equalize the capacity of the European powers to influence American affairs or even their intention of doing so. Toward France both the administration and the press expressed indifference. They regarded that power neither friend nor enemy. As the *National Intelligencer* (Washington) noted on May 4, 1815: "France is the same to us, whether ruled by Napoleon or Louis, by a King or an Emperor. — We owed no enmity to Louis; we own no debt of gratitude to Napoleon." The French government, fearful of British influence in the United States, anticipated considerable benefit from maintaining close and friendly ties with Washington. Shortly after the Congress of Vienna Adams reminded Monroe that such continental powers as France would attempt to separate the United States from England.[25] France itself posed no threat.

Russia, like France, seemed to lack the power or the intention to challenge American interest in the New World. Observant Americans recognized the contrast between the government and society of Russia and that of the United States, but they harbored no feeling of fear or distrust. Adams admitted that he trusted the Emperor Alexander more than any other monarch in Europe.[26] As a continental power with a large army, Russia wielded major influence in Europe and the Middle East; elsewhere Britain exerted a moderating influence on Russian ambition. Indeed, many Americans hoped — and Adams among them — that Anglo-Russian rivalry would restrict the power of both countries outside the Eastern Hemisphere.

Toward England the complacency which determined American attitudes toward the continent did not exist. England had the power, and seemingly the interest, to interfere in American affairs. Adams had taken hope in Napoleon's retention of power in France as a counterweight to British power.[27] There was little conviction in the United States after 1814 that England, having shaken off the restraints of France, would convert the Treaty of Ghent into an instrument of peace. Members of the press freely predicted renewed war, although not necessarily in the immediate future. As the *National Intelligencer* explained in April, 1816: "It has been predicted by our most perspecacious statesmen, that future wars of a sanguinary character are to take place between Great Britain and the U. States—These are events which, though perhaps as certain as mortality to man, it is agreeable to be enabled to believe are placed at a remote distance from us." Adams shared this post-war distrust of Britain. He wrote to his mother, Abigail, in December, 1815, that although British ascendancy in Europe would decline, that country would continue to seek the possible ruin of the United States. British animosity toward France had been satiated by the British victory, but warned Adams, "[British] feelings against America are keener, more jealous, more envious, more angry than ever."[28] Again he wrote, "We must not disguise from ourselves that the national feeling [in Britain] against the United States is more strong and universal than it has ever been."[29] Such fears did not govern United States policy toward Britain.

IV

For Adams peace with England was essential for American security and well being. Britain alone of Europe's leading states had the power to injure the United States. "My special duty at present," Adams wrote from London in May, 1816, "is to preach peace.... I am deeply convinced that peace is the state best adapted to the interest and happiness of both nations."[30] As secretary a year later he resumed negotiations on those issues, still unsettled since Ghent, which he had begun in London. As early as the peace negotiations of 1782 his father had sought the dismantling of all fortifications along the Canadian-American frontier. At Ghent in 1814 the younger Adams had pressed the British for such an agreement, but again without success. Still undaunted, Adams repeated the offer in London during March, 1816. The British government, hoping to avoid a naval race with the United States on the Great Lakes, accepted Adams' overture. The result was the Rush-Bagot Agreement, signed in Washington during April, 1817, which limited British and American naval arsenals on the lakes to those required for the enforcement of customs regulations. This treaty was the first reciprocal naval disarmament agreement in modern history. In removing a potential source of friction and expense, the treaty served the interests of both Britain and the United States admirably.[31]

During the following year Adams achieved the long-standing quest of the United States for fishing rights off the Labrador and

Newfoundland coasts. While in London Adams insisted that Britain had granted the inshore fisheries on the northern coasts to the United States in the original division of the Empire. The British agreed to American fishing on the high seas and suspended trespass proceedings against New England fishermen. In Washington Adams resumed his conversations on the fisheries question, determined to eliminate the English reference to "liberty" when referring to American access to both the Grand Banks and the high seas.[32] Privately Adams was opposed to compromise, preferring that the United States demand full American fishing rights along the northern coasts and establish them by force if necessary. Overruled by Monroe, Adams proposed that the United States forfeit the right of drying and curing on the shore and reserve full rights to fishing. Ultimately Albert Gallatin, who managed the final negotiations in 1818, achieved more extensive inshore fishing rights than Adams' instructions had demanded. The new treaty granted American fishermen permission not only to catch fish along extensive sections of the northern coasts but also to dry and cure fish on any of the unsettled coasts of Labrador. The British resisted the American effort to guarantee these fishing rights even in time of war but, as a compromise, they granted Americans liberty "for ever" to take fish along the northern coasts.[33]

As late as 1815 the United States and Britain had conducted a flourishing trade without benefit of any formal commercial treaty. On July 3 of that year Adams signed a commercial convention in London which, except for the prohibition of discriminatory duties, merely reaffirmed existing practice. The convention provided for reciprocal consulates, freedom of commerce between the United States and British territories in Europe, as well as equality of treatment of the products, ships, citizens, and subjects of each country in the ports of the other. The convention permitted American ships to trade in the British ports of Calcutta, Madras, Bombay, and Penang in south Asia.[34]

Unfortunately the Anglo-American convention of July, 1815, failed to gain full reciprocal arrangements, for Britain refused to permit American ships in the salt-water ports of British North America and the British West Indies. These restrictions, by permitting English traders to engage in a triangle traffic denied to Americans, cancelled the advantages of full reciprocity in direct United States-British commerce. For Adams this policy was totally objectionable. Commerce, he wrote, "being an interchange of commodities ... is just in itself. ... [T]he regulation of it should be by arrangements to which both parties consent and in which due regard is paid to the interests of both."[35]

Adams confronted the uncompromising London government with a series of congressional acts in 1817, 1818, and 1820 which imposed special tonnage dues on British ships entering the United States from ports denied to American vessels. Finally Congress eliminated all British West Indian goods except those brought directly from the colony where they were grown. These restrictions injured the West Indian economy and prompted Parliament, in 1822, to open some colonial ports to American ships. At the same time it enumerated American products which might compete with those of Canada. In March, 1823, Congress, under Adams' direction, opened United States ports to British ships coming from colonial ports, but only from those ports to which United States ships were admitted. At the same time Congress authorized the President to impose a 10 percent discriminatory tariff on colonial goods imported in British vessels until London eliminated all colonial preferences. By 1826 the British had again cut off American trade with their West Indian islands. Adams failed to negotiate conditions of greater reciprocity than those which existed in 1822.[36]

Adams pursued the principle of equal advantage for American merchants in France as well. That country was a special problem because of its discriminatory tariffs which favored goods shipped in French vessels over those arriving in foreign ships. What troubled Adams was not the legality of the French acts, but France's refusal to amend its restrictions reciprocally. In July, 1820, Congress inaugurated a trade war with France when it levied special duties on French bottoms. In Paris Albert Gallatin favored American acceptance of some French compromise proposal, convinced that United States vessels could compete favorably with the French against even the offered differential of $2.30 a ton. Monroe seemed to agree. But Adams insisted that the principle of reciprocity be maintained universally; Monroe rejected the French proposal. To terminate the quarrel, Paris dispatched its skilled diplomate, Baron Hyde de Neuville, to negotiate with Adams in Washington. Hyde de Neuville offered to remove half the French discriminatory duties if the United States removed its retaliatory tonnage dues. Adams opposed this compromise, but Monroe, under Gallatin's influence, relented. During subsequent months Gallatin secured further reductions of French discriminations. Finally in a treaty, accepted by the Senate in June, 1822, the two countries agreed to Adams' proposal of balanced discriminatory duties.[37] Although Adams for a time compromised his commercial principles, he managed ulti-mately to obtain better reciprocal arrangements with France than he did with England. The *National Intelligencer* of June 29, 1822, passed judgment on the French treaty: "It re-established relations of perfect amity with France, our old friend and ally, which have been somewhat disturbed by the recent collisions of the commer-cial regulations of the two countries. . . . " The French were equally pleased.

V

Even more spectacular was Adams' success in defining the boundaries of the Louisiana Purchase. In the Convention of 1818 with England he negotiated the boundary line from the Lake of the Woods westward along the 49th parallel to the Rocky Mountains. West of the Rockies, however, British fur-trading interests were centered south of that parallel, largely along the valley of the Columbia River. London, therefore, demanded the Columbia as the boundary between the mountains and the Pacific. Adams, who would settle for no less than a usable port along the Oregon shore, had been convinced by New England seamen that the Columbia River would never meet that need, largely because of the dangers of the bar that blocked its entrance. He understood also that the Strait of Juan de Fuca and Puget Sound, both north of the Columbia but south of 49°, constituted one of the world's best inland waterways. For these reasons Adams demanded no less than the extension of the 49th parallel to the Pacific. When British negotiators proved intractable on this point, Adams agreed to a policy of joint occupancy with Britain in the Oregon country west of the Rockies for a period of ten years, an arrangement which either country could terminate on one year's notice. Thus Adams delayed the final Oregon settlement until that time when the diplomatic advantage would pass to the United States.

Adams' subsequent diplomatic achievement, perhaps his greatest, came in 1819 when in the Adams-Onís Treaty he not only acquired Florida for the United States but also defined the southern bound-ary of the Louisiana Purchase from the Gulf of Mexico to the Pacific Ocean. Florida in 1817 was still under Spanish rule, but that region had become a problem for the United States government—and for the citizens of Georgia—simply because the Madrid regime was too plagued with political and military disor-ders elsewhere to maintain order in its colony. British adventurers in Florida perennially armed and incited the Florida Indians to raid north of the Florida boundary. Monroe dispatched General Andrew Jackson to punish the Indians for their destruction of American lives and property. Carrying out his instructions with considerable vigor, Jackson in 1818 pursued a band of marauding Indians into Florida where he captured and executed two British agents as well as two Indian chiefs. Spain protested the action. Jackson's enemies in Congress demanded the general's dismissal.

President Monroe and all members of the cabinet, except Adams, agreed. They argued that Jackson had exceeded his instructions and committed war against Spain, an act which required an official disavowal. Adams reminded the cabinet that Jackson's actions were defensive, that he had entered Florida, not to war on Spain, but to terminate the Indian depredations. Jackson had discretionary powers; to disavow them, believed Adams, was unthinkable. He admitted in his diary that he had pushed the case to the limit. "But," he added, "if the question was dubious, it was better to err on the side of vigor than of weakness—on the side of our own officer . . . than on the side of our bitterest enemies. . . . "[38] Adam's argument carried. On July 23, 1818, the secretary charged the complaining Spanish minister, Don Luis de Onis, that Spain had an obligation, under treaty, to keep order in Florida. The fort at St. Mark, Adams added, would be restored only to a Spanish force strong enough to hold it against an Indian attack. Peace between the United States and Spain, he warned, "requires that henceforth the stipulations by Spain to restrain by force her Indians from all hostilities against the United States should be faithfully and effectually fulfilled."[39] If Spain could not control the Indians, then it had no choice but to cede Florida to the United States. Castlereagh agreed with Adams.

Meanwhile on July 10, 1818, the French minister in Washington, Hyde de Neuville, informed Adams that Spain, recognizing its weakness, would cede Florida to the United States, provided that Washington assumed the claims of American citizens against Spain, estimated at some $5 million. Onis immediately took up the negotiations, raising the issue of the still-undefined southern boundary of the Louisiana Purchase. Spain hoped to push the line eastward and northward as far as possible; Adams sought a boundary which would bring as much of Texas and the Southwest as possible into the United States. Onis, on July 11, proposed a western boundary which would separate the United States from Spanish Mexico at a line moving northward between Adeas and

Natchitoches to the Red River and thence to the Missouri. Adams rejected this outright.[40] So uncompromising was Madrid that in October Adams threatened to break off the negotiations. Then on October 31 the secretary presented a note to Onis outlining what he termed the final United States offer:

> Beginning at the mouth of the River Sabine, on the Gulf of Mexico, following the course of said river to the thirty-second degree of latitude; the eastern bank and all the islands in said river to belong to the United States, and the western bank to Spain; thence, due north, to the northern-most part of the thirty-third degree of north latitude, and until it strikes the Rio Roxo, or Red River, thence, following the course of the said river, to its source, touching the chain of the Snow mountains, in latitude thirty-seven degrees twenty-five minutes north, longitude one hundred and six degrees fifteen minutes west, or thereabouts, as marked on Melish's map, thence to the summit of the said mountains, and following the chain of the same to the forty-first parallel of latitude; thence, following the said parallel of latitude forty-one degrees, to the South Sea. The northern bank of the said Red River, and all islands therein, to belong to the United States, and the southern bank of the same to Spain.

Through subsequent weeks the negotiations remained deadlocked. Then on January 3, 1819, Hyde de Neuville informed Adams that Onis had received new instructions which indicated a line extending to the Pacific at the 43rd parallel, but required a larger barrier for Santa Fe than Adams' Red River line would permit. But Onis, in January, demanded a line from the Missouri River to the mouth of the Columbia on the Pacific, sufficient, he said, to enable the United States to construct a system of internal communications from the Atlantic to the Pacific.[42] This line Adams rejected, but responded favorably to Madrid's request regarding Santa Fe. He altered his proposal of October 31, substituting for the Red River (to its mouth) a line to run due north from the Pawnee bend of the Red to the Arkansas, following that river to its source in the Rockies. From that point the line would run due north to 42°. When Adams, to his chagrin, discovered that Pawnee bend was four or five degrees west of his initial reading of 97° west longitude, he informed de Neuville that he preferred the 100th meridian. But he asked the French minister why Spain would demand four or five degrees of wilderness along the Pacific which would never be of value to it.

Thereafter Onis' counterproposals began to approach the American demands. On February 4 the French minister relayed Onis' acceptance of Adams' modified proposal along the Red with the substitution of the 43rd parallel for the 42nd along the Pacific. So close was the agreement that Monroe was inclined to concede all remaining points of conflict. Adams observed that "if Onis intends to conclude at all, we can obtain better." On February 12 Adams noted in his diary: "I am so constantly occupied and absorbed by this negotiation with Onis that almost all other business runs in arrear, and in a most especial manner this journal. I rode to the President's, and the adjourned Cabinet meeting was held. . . . I was finally authorized to accept the longitude one hundred from the Red to the Arkansas, and the latitude forty-three to the South Sea, if better cannot be obtained."[43]

By February 15 Onis had agreed to Adams' boundary, including the 42nd parallel, but insisted that the river lines follow the middle rather than the south bank of the streams. Adams countered that Spain would have no settlements near those rivers and that the middle of streams never lent themselves to precise lines of demarcation. Adams insisted before the cabinet that the United States adhere to the principle of owning the rivers and islands in them. On February 20 Onis capitulated, observing that Adams had given him more trouble than had the President. The Spanish minister recalled the words a suitor once addressed to Philip IV: "Sire, your Majesty has no influence with the Minister of Grace and Justice, for he refuses me what you have granted."[44]

On February 22, 1819, Onis and Adams signed the Trans-Continental Treaty. For Adams it was the capstone of his diplomatic career. "It was, perhaps," he wrote in his diary, "the most important day of my life. . . . May no disappointment embitter the hope which this event warrants us in cherishing, and may its future influence on the destinies of my country be as extensive and as favorable as our warmest anticipations can paint!"[45] Later members of Congress urged Adams to put the treaty aside and claim the Rio Grande. The secretary reminded one Congressman who came to criticise that he and Henry Clay were excellent negotiators in theory. Then he leveled a strong rebuke:

They were for obtaining all and granting nothing. They played a game between their own right and left hands, and could allot with admirable management the whole stake to one hand and total discomfiture to the other. In the negotiations with Spain we had a just claim to the Mississippi and its waters, and our citizens had a fair though very precarious claim to indemnities. We had a mere color of claim to the Rio del Norte, no claim to a line beyond the Rocky Mountains, and none to Florida, which we very much wanted. The treaty . . . barely gives up to Spain the colorable claim from the Sabine to the Rio del Norte. Now, negotiation implies some concession upon both sides. If after obtaining every object of your pursuit but one, and that one weak in principle and of no present value, what would you have offered to Spain to yield that also?[46]

The Congressman had no answer.

VI

Spain's challenge to the United States lay not only in that nation's weakness in Florida but also in its precarious position throughout the Western Hemisphere. Napoleon's invasion of Spain in 1808 had terminated Madrid's effective control of Spanish America. Provisional *juntas* maintained by Spain's ruling classes continued to claim jurisdiction over the Empire, but by 1812 their New World influence was purely nominal. Freed of Spain's commercial restrictions, the various regions of Latin America opened their commerce to the world. British and Yankee shippers entered South American ports in large numbers. When war broke out between the restored Spanish monarchy and the now-rebellious colonies, the struggling South Americans looked to the United States especially for economic, military, and moral support.

Within the United States editors, Congressmen, and administration officials favored Latin American independence with almost total unanimity. On the proper national response to Latin America's plight there was no agreement at all. Abbe de Pradt, the prolific European writer, emphasized not only the importance of Latin America to Europe but also the possibility that, inasmuch as Spanish control was doomed, the great European powers might establish the region's independence on terms that would keep the new nations attached to Europe. Determined to sever Europe's ties with the New World, editors led by William Duane of Philadelphia's *Aurora* demanded United States guardianship of Latin American independence. In Latin America, argued Duane, this nation would find "the corrective of European jealousy, and the resources with which to defeat and counterplace the intolerant and malignant selfishness of European nations."[47] In Congress the powerful Clay denounced the administration for neglecting American interests and the cause of liberty.

Monroe and Adams would not be stampeded. They recognized the overwhelming preference of United States citizens for Latin American independence, but they refused to commit the United States before the European powers had revealed their intentions or the patriots of South America had demonstrated their capacity to establish their independence and maintain a semblance of order. Adams was appalled at the open congressional support for Latin America. "There seemed to me," he complained in June, 1816, "too much of the warlike humor in the debates of Congress — propositions even to take up the cause of the South Americans; predictions of wars with this country to the end of time, as cool and as causeless, as if they were talking of the expense of building a light house. . . . "[48]

As the public pressure for involvement continued, Adams reminded his father in December, 1817, that Latin America had replaced the French Revolution as the great source of discord in the United States: "The republican spirit of our country not only sympathizes with people struggling in a cause, . . . but it is working into indignation against the relapse of Europe into the opposite principle of monkery and despotism. And now, as at the early stage of the French Revolution, we have ardent spirits who are for rushing into the conflict, without looking to the consequences."[49] Adams doubted that the people of South America were capable of self-government; thus he viewed the revolutions with little sympathy. Monroe, somewhat more sympathetic, argued that the United States could render Latin Americans no service more useful than to refrain from any action which might provoke direct European intervention. He explained his views in a letter to Jackson in December, 1818, although later he omitted the key passage: "By this policy we have lost nothing, as *by keeping the Allies out of the quarrel,* Florida must soon be ours, and *the Colonies must be independent, for if they cannot beat Spain, they do not deserve to be free.*"[50]

During 1818 the ultimate course of United States policy toward Latin America began to emerge. In March, Monroe requested a congressional appropriation to defray the expenses of a commission of inquiry to South America. Clay attached an amendment appropriating $18,000 for a United States legation in Buenos Aires, thereby to compel the administration to recognize the independence of the Argentine. Clay stepped down from the Speaker's rostrum to enter a strong plea for his measure, but the House remained unconvinced and voted down the amendment, 115 to 45. Shortly thereafter Adams expressed his contempt for Congress in his diary: "The present session will stand remarkable in the annals of the Union for showing how a legislature can keep itself employed when having nothing to do. . . . The proposed appropriation for a minister to Buenos Ayres has gone the way of other things lost upon earth, like the purchase of oil for light houses in the western country." In July the President's fact-finding commission returned to Washington, hopelessly divided.[51] Still the administration continued to respond to changing conditions both in Europe and in Latin America. By the summer of 1818 Monroe and Adams concluded that the great European states would never agree on measures to restore Spanish sovereignty in South America, especially since Britain clearly favored independence. At the Conference of Aix-la-Chapelle, which opened in September, 1818, England opposed the use of force against the Latin Americans. But Castlereagh's rejection of Adams' suggestion for a concerted British-American policy encouraged further caution in Washington.

Through 1819 and 1820 Adams moved slowly and deliberately, proclaiming official American neutrality toward the struggles of Latin America. He reminded Monroe that any successful revolution reaches a stage when those fighting for independence merit recognition, and when recognition is no longer a departure from the obligations of neutrality. Still, Adams continued, "The justice of a cause . . . is not sufficient to justify third parties in siding with it."[52] Finally in February, 1821, ratified copies of the Trans-Continental Treaty were exchanged in Washington. This eliminated the one remaining international argument against recognition of Latin American independence. That year the striking victories of the revolutionary forces all but destroyed Spain's remaining authority in South America. Clay secured passage of two resolutions in the House, one expressing interest in South American independence, the other encouraging the President to recognize the independence of the new nations whenever he believed it expedient. Shortly thereafter, in March, 1821, Clay and Adams discussed Latin America at length, each regretting their years of deep disagreement. Adams again argued the administration's case for delay.

> That the final issue of their present struggle would be their entire independence of Spain [he informed Clay] I have never doubted. That it was our true policy and duty to take no part in the contest I was equally clear. . . . So far as they were contending for independence, I wished well to their cause; but I had seen and yet see no prospect that they would establish free or liberal institutions of government. They are not likely to promote the spirit either of freedom or order by their example. They have not the first elements of good or free government. Arbitrary power, military and ecclesiastical, was stamped upon their education, upon their habits, and upon all their institutions. Civil dissension was infused into all their seminal principles. War and mutual destruction was in every member of their organization, moral, political, and physical. I had little expectation of any beneficial result to this country from any future connection with them, political or commercial. We should derive no improvement to our own institutions by any communion with theirs. Nor was there any appearance of a disposition in them to take any political lesson from us. As to the commercial connection, I agreed with him that little weight should be allowed to arguments of mere pecuniary interest; but there was no basis for much traffic between us. They want none of our productions, and we could afford to purchase very few of theirs.[53]

Monroe recognized the changing conditions in a special message to Congress on March 8, 1822. He declared that Chile, the United Provinces of the Plata (Argentina), Peru, Colombia, and Mexico were fully independent and thus could rightfully claim recognition by other nations. Congress responded by appropriating funds to meet the expense of "such missions to the independent nations on the American continent as the President might deem proper." Following formal recognition of the five new states, Latin American representatives added both numbers and variety to the Washington diplomatic corps.

Further delay, Monroe explained to Madison, would have produced deep resentment in Latin America and opened the way for renewed European encroachments. Even as Monroe sought the exclusion of European influence from the Western Hemisphere he reassured the European powers that the United States had no intention to control the new governments or to create a separate American system. Neither Monroe nor Adams revealed much concern for the nature of the Latin American regimes. Nor did they favor the immediate assignment of ministers to the new capitals. No commercial treaties, based on reciprocity, could possibly affect Britain's dominance of Latin America's foreign trade. "As to running a race with England to snatch from these new nations some special privilege or monopoly," admitted Adams, "I thought it neither a wise nor an honest policy."[54]

VII

Britain made clear its deep commercial and political preference for Latin American independence at the Conference of Aix-la-Chapelle in 1818. Still George Canning, Britain's foreign minister after September, 1822, out of deference to Spain and the Holy Alliance, refused to follow the American lead. So guarded had been Monroe's recognition policy that it produced no break with Spain. British policy, unlike that in Washington, focused on Europe, especially when the Holy Alliance, over London's objection, voted to send a French army into Spain to put down a liberal revolt. When in 1822 the invading French successfully restored Ferdinand VII to his full royal prerogatives in Spain, Canning suspected that France might attempt to restore the Spanish Empire as well. Even more threatening was the possibility that France might use its influence in Spain to lay the foundation for another French empire in America. Early in 1823, the British minister warned the Paris government against any move to acquire portions of Spanish America by conquest or cession. When French policy in Spain continued to cause unease in London, Canning, in August, turned to Richard Rush, the American minister. He suggested that Britain and the United States issue a joint declaration disavowing any territorial ambitions in Latin America but warning Europe, except Spain itself, against intervention.

Rush was highly flattered by Canning's recognition of America's growing importance in the Atlantic world, but insisted on referring the matter to Washington unless Britain recognized the independence of the Latin American nations immediately. This Canning refused to do. Instead, he delivered a secret warning to Paris.

The French government responded with the famed "Polignac Memorandum" which assured the British that it had no intention of dispatching an expedition to the New World. Thus Canning, through unilateral action, had resolved the immediate challenge to British policy.

Rush, in a long communication of August 19, 1823, relayed Canning's proposal to Washington. Monroe received the dispatch on October 9. He did not regard Europe threatening; still he favored Canning's proposition and sought reassurance from his old friend Jefferson, in quiet retirement at Monticello. Jefferson, in a classic response, reiterated his concept of the two spheres which advocated the noninterference of the United States in European affairs and the noninvolvement of Europe in the affairs of the New World. For Jefferson it was imperative that this country, if it desired to maintain the *status quo* in the Western Hemisphere, not take a stand against the existing order in Europe.[55] Only one nation—Britain—could challenge American interests in the New World; it was the part of wisdom, therefore, to enlist that great power in the cause of emancipating the American continents from European influence. Madison likewise endorsed Canning's proposal.

Meanwhile Adams had responded to the French invasion of Spain by reasserting the doctrine of *no-transfer*. France's policy in Spain was not Adams' major concern. What troubled him was the possibility that Spain might cede Cuba to Britain as the price of an Anglo-Spanish alliance. In April, 1823, Adams sent a long note to Hugh Nelson, the American minister in Madrid, warning the Spanish government that the United States would oppose the transfer of Cuba to any European power. Such a transfer, wrote Adams, would not only affect Spanish-American relations but also subvert the rights of the Cuban people and justify the United States in supporting any resulting independence movement.[56] When Canning assured Washington that Britain had no intention of acquiring the island, Monroe suggested to the cabinet that the United States issue a statement of self-denial also. Adams objected; for him there was no reason for the United States to bind itself permanently against the possibility that Cuba might one day solicit union with the United States.[57] Monroe assured London informally that the United States also had no designs on Cuba.

Russia had also posed a threat to United States interest in the Western Hemisphere and provoked another historic response from Adams. Before the 1820's rumors of Russian encroachment along the Pacific coast of North America as far south as California had produced only indifference in Washington. To Adams Russia lacked both the navy and the merchant marine to establish distant colonies.[58] But in 1821 the Russian Emperor issued a ukase which excluded foreigners from trading, fishing, or navigating within one hundred Italian miles of the northwest coast from Bering Straits to the 51st parallel of north latitude. Both Britain and the United States objected. At a cabinet meeting on June 28, 1823, Adams introduced the question of Russian claims. These, he believed, the United States should contest, especially since that country had no settlements in the disputed region. On July 17, Adams informed Baron Tuyl, the Russian minister, that the United States would contest the right of Russia to any territorial establishment on this continent, and that this nation assumed the principle that "the American continents are no longer subject for *any* new European colonial establishments."[59] On July 22 he penned a note to Middleton in St. Petersburg: "There can, perhaps, be no better time for saying, frankly and explicitly, to the Russian Government that the future peace of the world, and the interest of Russia herself, can not be promoted by Russian settlements upon any part of the American continent. With the exception of the British establishments north of the United States, the remainder of both the American continents must henceforth be left to the management of American hands."[60] Thus Adams asserted the principle of *non colonization.*

When Monroe returned to Washington with the opinions of Jefferson and Madison corroborating his own, Russia had created another crisis. Baron Tuyl warned Adams that the Tsar would not recognize the new governments of Latin America and that, unless the United States remained neutral, Russia might support a European invasion of the former Spanish Empire. This Russian threat merely confirmed those convictions in Washington that Canning's proposal should be accepted. But Adams refused to be frightened. He doubted that France intended armed intervention in Latin America; moreover, the British navy was powerful enough to prevent it. The secretary suspected that Canning's overture was aimed less at obtaining unnecessary United States support than in preventing, though a self-denying agreement, future American expansion into Texas and the Caribbean. When the cabinet met on November 7, Adams proposed that the United States decline the British overture and take its stand against the Holy Alliance unilaterally. "It would be more candid, as well as more dignified," he said, "to avow our principles explicitly to Russia and

France, than to come in as a cock-boat in the wake of the British man-of-war."[61]

Adams favored an over-all American policy that would combine a letter to Russia with one to France in a single statement of national intent. To this Monroe agreed. Still the President hesitated to reject the British proposal. The news that France had captured Cadiz caused him to despair for the future of South America. Calhoun, equally fearful of Europe, proposed that Rush be given discretionary power to accept Canning's overture, if necessary. Adams argued that Spain had no more power to restore its control in the Western Hemisphere than had Chimborazo to sink to the bottom of the sea. "But," Adams warned, "if the South Americans were really in a state to be so easily subdued, it would be but a more forcible motive for us to beware of involving ourselves in their fate."[62]

A week later Adams delivered his note to the Russian minister. In moderate language he explained that the United States was a republic and thus was attracted to the Latin American states by those very principles which repelled the Tsar. He hoped that Russia would maintain its policy of neutrality. But Russia quickly created further alarm when another note reminded the United States of the Holy Alliance's success in putting down revolutions in Europe and its obligation to guarantee tranquility everywhere, including Latin America. As gloom settled over the Potomac, Adams told the cabinet:

> My purpose would be in a moderate and conciliatory manner, but with a firm and determined spirit, to declare our dissent from the principles avowed in those communications; to assert those upon which our own Government is founded, and while disclaiming all . . . interference with the political affairs of Europe, to declare our expectation and hope that the European powers will equally abstain from the attempt to spread their principles in the American hemisphere, or to subjugate by force any part of these continents to their will.

Adams thus formulated the principle of *hands-off;* Monroe accepted it and decided to proclaim this new American purpose toward the Western Hemisphere in his December message to Congress.

On November 21, Monroe read a preliminary draft of his forthcoming message to the cabinet. Adams was shocked. "Its introduction," he recorded, "was in a tone of deep solemnity and of high alarm, intimating that this country is menaced by imminent and formidable dangers, such as would probably soon call for their most vigorous energies and the closest union." What distressed Adams especially was Monroe's reversion to his old Republican innocence in taking up the cause of revolution in Spain and Greece— two areas in which he had no intention of acting. He asked the President to reconsider the entire subject.

> This message [said Adams] would be a summons to arms—to arms against all Europe, and for objects of policy exclusively European—Greece and Spain. It would be as new, too, in our policy as it would be surprising. For more than thirty years Europe had been in convulsions; every nation almost of which it is composed alternately invading and invaded. Empires, kingdoms, principalities, had been overthrown, revolutionized, and counterrevolutionized, and we had looked on safe in our distance beyond an intervening ocean, and avowing a total forbearance to interfere in any of the combinations of European politics. This message would at once buckle on the harness and throw down the gauntlet. It would have the air of open defiance to all Europe, and I should not be surprised if the first answer to it from Spain and France, and even Russia, should be to break off their diplomatic intercourse with us. I did not expect that the quiet which we had enjoyed for six or seven years would last much longer. The aspect of things was portentous; but if we must come to an issue with Europe, let us keep it off as long as possible. Let us use all possible means to carry the opinion of the nation with us, and the opinion of the world.[63]

Adams was especially disturbed at Monroe's open endorsement of the Greek independence movement, for he had long argued against United States involvement in that cause. The Greek revolutionary movement had slowly gathered strength until by 1821 it posed an immediate threat to Ottoman rule. Sultan Mahmud II retaliated with such violence and destruction that he aroused anti-Turkish sentiment throughout western Europe and the United States. In 1822 *Niles' Register*, dwelling on Turkish barbarities, chided the country for not taking up the cause of Greek liberty and independence. In his annual message of December, 1822, Monroe expressed regret that a country which had contributed so much to

121

civilization should live under a gloomy despotism. Still concern for the Greek cause languished. Then in 1823 Edward Everett, professor of Greek literature at Harvard and editor of *The North American Review,* championed Greek independence and enlisted the support of Daniel Webster.[64] Adams was not impressed. He argued strongly against any American meddling in the affairs of Greece and Turkey, especially since the country was not prepared financially or militarily to intervene. When Crawford and Calhoun in the cabinet expressed great enthusiasm for the Greeks, Adams recorded his disgust:

> Mr. Gallatin had proposed in one of his last dispatches, as if he was serious, that we should assist the Greeks with our naval force in the Mediterranean—one frigate, one corvette, and one schooner. Mr. Crawford and Mr. Calhoun inclined to countenance this project. Crawford asked, hesitatingly, whether we were at peace with Turkey, and seemed only to wait for opposition to maintain that we were not. Calhoun descanted upon his great enthusiasm for the cause of the Greeks; he was for taking no heed of Turkey whatever. In this, as in many other cases, these gentlemen have two sources of eloquence at these Cabinet meetings—one with reference to sentiment, and the other to action. Their enthusiasm for the Greeks is all sentiment, and the standard of this is the prevailing popular feeling. As for action, they are seldom agreed; and after two hours of discussion this day the subject was dismissed, leaving it precisely where it was—nothing determined, and nothing practicable proposed by either of them.[65]

Amid the critical cabinet debates on the President's message during late November, Adams again passed judgment on the Greek issue and the motives of those who favored it:

> I called at the President's, and found Mr. Gallatin with him. He still adhered to his idea of sending a naval force and a loan of money to the Greeks; and as he is neither an enthusiast nor a fool, and knows perfectly well that no such thing will be done, I look for the motives of this strange proposal, and find them not very deeply laid. Mr. Gallatin still builds castles in the air of popularity and, being under no responsibility for consequences,

patronizes the Greek cause for the sake of raising his reputation. His measure will not succeed, and even if it should, all the burden and danger of it will not bear upon him, but upon the Administration, and he will be the great champion of Grecian liberty.[66]

For Adams it was essential that Monroe not antagonize the Holy Alliance needlessly. If the European powers chose to challenge the United States, Washington should meet the issue but not create it. If the Holy Alliance really intended to restore the colonies to Spain, which Adams doubted, the United States had perhaps been too hasty in acknowledging South American independence. Earlier the administration had not even thought of interfering in the affairs of Europe. "If they intend now to interpose by force," Adams warned, "we shall have as much as we can do to prevent them, without going to bid them defiance in the heart of Europe." Arguing steadily against any American involvement in European affairs, Adams summarized his views before the cabinet: "The ground that I wish to take is that of earnest remonstrance against the interference of the European powers by force with South America, but to disclaim all interference on our part with Europe; to make an American cause, and adhere inflexibly to that." Adams had added to hands-off his principle of *abstention*.

This concept of two worlds Monroe embodied in his celebrated message to Congress on December 2, 1823. The so-called Monroe Doctrine declared specifically that the American continents were no longer open to European colonization and that the United States would regard any effort of the European powers to extend their government to any portion of the Western Hemisphere as a threat to its peace and safety. On the other hand, Monroe assured the nations of the Old World that the United States would not interfere with their dependencies in the New World or involve itself in matters purely European. Meanwhile Adams prepared documents to Britain and Russia. He assured Canning that the United States intended to pursue separate, but parallel, policies in Latin America. Together Adams and Monroe had wedded American policies to the *status quo* in the Atlantic, a *status quo* which, if threatened, would have the defense of the British navy itself. Adams' communication to Russia concluded with a strong warning against European interference in the affairs of the Western Hemisphere. The secretary regarded this dispatch, dated November 27, 1823, as the most important state paper of his career.[67]

Early in 1824 Adams resolved the far Northwest conflict with Russia. New England traders demanded access to the fur-seals and sea-otters in the Aleutians far north of 51°. Adams reminded Stratford Canning in Washington that the United States had no territorial claims as far north as the 51st parallel, and assumed that British interests would be sufficient to counter Russian demands. To Russia Adams suggested a boundary at 55° north latitude. In St. Petersburg the Russian government accepted Adams' non-colonization principle as well as the American right of access to unsettled regions north of the line of division. To keep all of Prince of Wales Island under Russian control, the Russians proposed the boundary of 54° 40'. In the Convention of April, 1824, Russia gained its preferred boundary but gave up all pretensions to a *mare clausum* in the north Pacific.[68]

Even as the April convention disposed of the Russian threat in the far Northwest Adams' allies laid the Greek issue to rest in Congress. These triumphs for the concept of two worlds as embodied in the Monroe Doctrine were the last of Adams' secretarial years. Through eight years it was Adams' recognition of geographic factors as the foundation of national interests and diplomatic advantage that underlay his varied goals and successes. Adams detected more assuredly than his contemporaries that European influence in the Western Hemisphere was declining. This assumption encouraged his anticipation of Latin American independence, his vision of an expanding republic on the North American continent, and his disinclination to compromise on issues purely American. Recognizing the limits of United States power outside the Western Hemisphere, he argued against all verbal commitments that transcended easily-demonstrable national interests or any intention of the government to act. Adams understood that such involvements served no national requirements and ultimately disappointed everyone who took the rhetoric seriously. Rejecting the need of threats or war, he settled for what diplomacy could accomplish. Where he possessed the diplomatic advantage, as in the Rush-Bagot and Adams-Onis treaties, he pursued the American interest as he defined it. Where the nation's advantage was doubtful, as on the questions of Oregon and commercial reciprocity, he either postponed the settlement until the superior interests and advantages of the United States became apparent or simply accepted less than he desired. Where the issue was revolution in Latin American, Greece, or Spain, he abstained from involvement totally. The essence of Adams's statesmanship was his ability to define a clear hierarchy of national interests to be pursued. Adams never permitted his objectives to outrun the means available to him.

Adams's diplomatic achievements were remarkable. What he had contributed to the nation's thought was less tangible but no less impressive. But Adams' ultimate purpose transcended even such triumphs and looked rather to some lasting contribution to the good of the world. Referring to a projected convention for establishing neutral and belligerent rights in wartime, he confided to his diary:

> When I think, if it possibly could succeed, what a real and solid blessing it would be to the human race, I can scarcely guard myself from a spirit of enthusiasm, which it becomes me to distrust. I feel that I could die for it with joy, and that if my last moments could be cheered with the consciousness of having contributed to it, I could go before the throne of Omnipotence with a plea for mercy, and with a consciousness of not having lived in vain for the world of mankind.[69]

NOTES

1. John Quincy Adams, "Marcellus" Papers, in *Writings of John Quincy Adams,* ed. Worthington C. Ford (New York, 1913-1917), I, 135-46.
2. *Memoirs of John Quincy Adams,* ed. Charles Francis Adams (Philadelphia, 1874-1877), V, 135-36.
3. October 12, 1818, *ibid.,* IV, 131-32.
4. Quoted in Samuel Flagg Bemis, *John Quincy Adams and the Foundations of American Foreign Policy* (New York, 1949), p. 253. Adams complained that dinners and evening parties resulted in late hours and caused him to lose the mornings which followed as well as the evenings themselves. See *Memoirs of John Quincy Adams,* IV, 279-80.
5. Bemis, *John Quincy Adams,* p. 243.
6. *Ibid.,* pp. 260-261.
7. Adams to Abigail Adams, April 23, 1817, *Writings of John Quincy Adams,* VI, 182.
8. *Memoirs of John Quincy Adams,* VI, 171.
9. Hyde de Neuville to Richelieu, December 11, 1817, quoted in Edward H. Tatum, Jr., *The United States and Europe, 1815-1823* (Berkeley, Calif., 1936), pp. 208-09.
10. Adams to Alexander H. Everett, March 16, 1816, *Writings of John Quincy Adams,* V, 538; Adams to William Eustis, March 29, 1816, *ibid.,* V, 546.

11. *Memoirs of John Quincy Adams,* V, 173.
12. *Ibid.,* V, 112.
13. Quoted in Stanley Lane-Poole, *Life of Stratford Canning* (London, 1888), I, 308.
14. *Memoirs of John Quincy Adams,* V, 47-48.
15. Adams to John Adams, August 1, 1816, *Writings of John Quincy Adams,* VI, 60-62.
16. Adams to Joseph Hall, September 9, 1815, *ibid.,* V, 376-77.
17. This speech can be found in Walter LaFeber, ed., *John Quincy Adams and American Continental Empire* (Chicago, 1965), pp. 42-46.
18. *Memoirs of John Quincy Adams,* IV, 437-39.
19. *Ibid.,* V, 252-53.
20. Adams to Abigail Adams, January 17, 1814, *Writings of John Quincy Adams,* V, p. 5; Adams to Monroe, November 20, 1814, *ibid.,* V, 202.
21. Adams to William Harris Crawford, September 14, 1814, *ibid.,* V, 140-41; Adams to Alexander H. Everett, March 16, 1816, *ibid.,* V, 537; Adams to John Adams, February 17, 1814, *ibid.,* V, 18.
22. For a brilliant analysis of the requirements of a postwar European equilibrium see Charles Maurice de Talleyrand to Metternich, December 19, 1814, in Moorhead Wright, ed., *Theory and Practice of the Balance of Power,* 1486-1914 (Dent, London, 1975), pp. 99-104.
23. C. J. Bartlett, *Castlereagh* (New York, 1966), pp. 262-63. This excellent study evaluates the problems of British diplomacy in the years after the Congress of Vienna.
24. For Adams' view of European reaction see Adams to Samuel Dexter, April 14, 1816, *Writings of John Quincy Adams,* VI, 15.
25. Adams to Monroe, September 5, 1815, *ibid.,* V, 370.
26. Adams to Abigail Adams, May 12, 1814, *ibid.,* V, 43.
27. Adams to John Adams, April 24, 1815, *ibid.,* V, 309.
28. Adams to Abigail Adams, December 27, 1815, *ibid.,* V, 454.
29. Quoted in Arthur P. Whitaker, *The United States and the Independence of Latin America, 1800-1830* (Baltimore, 1941), p. 206.
30. Adams to John Adams, May 29, 1816, *Writings of John Quincy Adams,* VI, 38.
31. See Bemis, *John Quincy Adams,* pp. 230-31.
32. *Ibid.,* pp. 234-35.
33. *Ibid.,* pp. 279-80, 290-91.
34. *Ibid.,* pp. 224-25, 227.
35. Memorandum to Hyde de Neuville, April 26, 1821, *Writings of John Quincy Adams,* VII, 101-02.
36. Bemis, *John Quincy Adams,* pp. 457-59, 465.
37. *Ibid.,* pp. 450-53, 455-56.
38. *Memoirs of John Quincy Adams,* IV, 113.
39. *American State Papers, Foreign Relations,* IV, 497-99.
40. July 10, 11, 1818, *Memoirs of John Quincy Adams,* IV, 106-07.

41. October 26, 1818, *Memoirs of John Quincy Adams,* IV, 144; Adams to Onis, October 31, 1818, *Writings of John Quincy Adams,* VI, 457-58.
42. January 3, 15, 1819, *Memoirs of John Quincy Adams,* IV, 208-10, 218-19.
43. February 4, 11, 12, 1819, *ibid.,* IV, 244, 249-53.
44. February 15, 18, 19, 20, 1819, *ibid.,* IV, 255, 264, 267-68, 270.
45. February 22, 1819, *ibid.,* IV, 274-75.
46. *Ibid.,* V, 68-69.
47. See Whitaker, *United States and the Independence of Latin America,* pp. 104-12.
48. Adams to George William Erving, June 10, 1816, *Writings of John Quincy Adams,* VI, 45.
49. Adams to John Adams, December 21, 1817, *ibid.,* VI, 275-76.
50. Quoted in Whitaker, *United States and the Independence of Latin America,* pp. 210-11.
51. *Memoirs of John Quincy Adams,* IV, 155-56.
52. Adams to George William Erving, April 20, 1818, *Writings of John Quincy Adams,* VI, 309; Adams to Monroe, August 24, 1818, *ibid.,* VI, 442-43.
53. *Memoirs of John Quincy Adams,* V, 324-25.
54. June 20, 1822, *ibid.,* VI, 24-25.
55. See Tatum, *United States and Europe,* pp. 262-64.
56. Adams to Hugh Nelson, April 28, 1823, *Writings of John Quincy Adams,* VII, 381.
57. *Ibid.,* p. 373.
58. Adams to George Washington Campbell, June 28, 1818, *ibid.,* VI, 372.
59. *Memoirs of John Quincy Adams,* VI, 163.
60. *American State Papers, Foreign Relations,* V, 443, 445.
61. *Memoirs of John Quincy Adams,* VI, 177, 180-81.
62. November 13, 1823, *ibid.,* VI, 185-86.
63. November 21, 1823, *ibid.,* VI, 194-95.
64. For an excellent survey of United States reaction to the Greek revolution see Myrtle A. Cline, *American Attitudes Toward the Greek War of Independence, 1821-1828* (Atlanta, Ga., 1930), pp. 9-35.
65. *Memoirs of John Quincy Adams,* VI, 172-73.
66. November 24, 1823, *ibid.,* VI, 198-99.
67. *Ibid.,* VI, 211-12.
68. See Bemis, *John Quincy Adams,* pp. 514-15, 523-24.
69. *Memoirs of John Quincy Adams,* VI, 166.

6

DANIEL WEBSTER AND
AMERICAN CONSERVATISM

Kenneth E. Shewmaker

Daniel Webster is generally known as one of the greatest lawyers, orators, and politicians of nineteenth-century America, and he possesses an equally outstanding reputation as a diplomatist. In the basic work on the office of secretary of state, Alexander De Conde ranked Webster among the top ten secretaries of state in American history, and a recent poll of historians of American foreign policy upheld that high standing.[1] Webster served two terms as secretary of state under three presidents. From March 6, 1841 to May 8, 1843, he functioned as the chief cabinet officer to William Henry Harrison and John Tyler. On July 23, 1850, he became the first to hold a nonconsecutive term as secretary of state, and he continued as Millard Fillmore's principal adviser on foreign affairs until his death on October 24, 1852. While Webster was deferential toward all of the presidents under whom he worked, his was the dominant voice in the formulation, implementation, and interpretation of American foreign policy from 1841 to 1843 and from 1850 to 1852.

The purpose of this essay is to evaluate Webster's leadership in the field of foreign affairs in terms of thought and action. Webster was an eminently pragmatic statesman, and he did not tend to philosophize about issues. He left no memoirs, believing, as he wrote in 1851, that "Public men and scholars will be remembered by their works."[2] It is, then, more difficult to assess his thought than it is to appraise his actions. Nevertheless, it can be said that

129

Webster approached the world in which he lived with a set of assumptions and principles that added up to what might be called a conservative philosophy of international relations.

There were five major aspects to Webster's conservative philosophy. The first was a respect for the traditions of American foreign policy. By the time Webster became secretary of state, the United States had developed a set of policy guidelines. The most important of these grew out of the Neutrality Act of June 5, 1794, George Washington's Farewell Address of September 17, 1796, Congress's No-Transfer Resolution of January 15, 1811, and James Monroe's message of December 2, 1823. Washington had been Webster's boyhood idol, and he adhered throughout his career to the tenets of isolationism, as defined by national interest, and neutrality that took form during Washington's presidency. For example, when the Fillmore administration's conscientious efforts failed to prevent Narciso López from launching a filibustering expedition against Cuba from American soil in 1851, Webster graciously apologized to the Spanish government for the breach of neutrality. In a letter dated November 13, 1851, to Calderón de la Barca, minister of Spain to the United States, he denounced the actions taken against Spanish citizens as "disgraceful," expressed regret for any indignities to the Spanish flag, that gallant "Castilian ensign, which, in times past, has been reared so high, and waved so often over fields of acknowledged and distinguished valor," and promised to seek indemnity for the Spanish consul of New Orleans, whose consulate had been ransacked by a disorderly mob.[3] When Britain and France subsequently proposed a tripartite convention guarantying Cuba to Spain, Webster reminded them of the traditional American policy of isolationism. The United States, he wrote on April 29, 1852, had uniformly sought "to avoid as far as possible alliances or agreements with other States, and to keep itself free from national obligations, except such as affect directly the interests of the United States themselves."[4]

First elected to Congress in 1812, Webster also was fully aware of the no-transfer principle and became an early defender of what came to be known as the Monroe Doctrine. On January 14, 1843, in response to rumors that British officials in Cuba were intriguing to foment a revolution, Webster strongly reiterated the no-transfer policy, even stating that the Tyler administration was prepared to use military force if necessary to prevent the establishment of a British protectorate over the strategically-located island.[5] As early as 1826, in a speech delivered before the House of Representatives,

Webster called Monroe's "declaration" a national "treasure of reputation" and vowed "to guard it."[6] In the so-called Tyler Doctrine of 1842, which was authored by Webster, he extended Monroe's principles of noncolonization and nonintervention to the Hawaiian islands.[7] Webster's thinking about international relations, then, was strongly influenced by what he perceived to be the wisdom of the Founding Fathers.

Legalism and constitutionalism were also facets of Webster's conservatism. One of the most respected lawyers of his time, Webster was renowned for his legal expertise and knowledge of constitutional law. He also was well versed in the law of nations. As a young man, he had studied under the prestigious international jurist Christopher Gore, and, beginning with maritime cases growing out of the War of 1812, he gained an extensive understanding of international law through his own legal practice. This background helps to explain the enduring contributions to international jurisprudence that Webster made while serving as secretary of state, the most noteworthy being the important doctrine of self-defense that he set forth in 1841 in relation to the *Caroline* dispute with Britain. In 1837, Canadian military forces had crossed the Niagara River and destroyed the steamer *Caroline,* which was moored at Schlosser, New York. The British government justified this violation of American territorial sovereignty on the grounds of self-defense, the *Caroline* being a notorious gun-runner which provided arms and munitions to Canadian rebels under the leadership of William L. Mackenzie. In a note of April 24, 1841 to Henry S. Fox, the British minister to the United States, Webster argued that such incursions would be legitimate only if a government could "show a necessity of self-defence, instant, overwhelming, leaving no choice of means, and no moment for deliberation."[8] He thereby made a lasting impact on international law. In 1945–46, the Nuremberg Tribunal expressly endorsed Webster's doctrine of self-defense, and it continues to be the norm by which so-called acts of self-defense are assessed. In 1976, the Israelis drew upon Webster's views to justify their raid at the Entebbe airport in Uganda, and in 1981 the representative of Uganda to the Security Council of the United Nations denounced Israel's bombardment of Iraq's nuclear research station at Tuwaitha as a violation of Webster's classic formulation of the right of self-defense.[9]

When it came to the federal government's constitutional authority in the realm of foreign policy, Webster took a Hamiltonian view. The main problem in antebellum America was not a struggle between the executive and the legislative over the war power, which Webster and the presidents under whom he served conceded to Congress, but over intrusions by state governments in international relations. The first crisis that Webster faced as secretary of state in 1841 involved the strange case of Alexander McLeod, which John Quincy Adams aptly summarized as "that wretched question about the State right of New York to hang McLeod."[10] On November 12, 1840, McLeod, a Canadian deputy sheriff, had been arrested in Lewiston, New York, and charged with murder and arson in connection with the *Caroline* incident. The Van Buren administration took the position that it could do nothing to interfere in the legal processes of the sovereign state of New York, and Lord Palmerston, the fiery British foreign secretary, truculently threatened on February 9, 1841, that "McLeod's execution would produce war; war immediate and frightful in its character, because it would be a war of retaliation and vengeance."[11]

With responsible observers on both sides of the Atlantic predicting a third Anglo-American war, Webster reversed the policy of his predecessor, John Forsyth, and accepted the British contention that since those involved in the raid upon the *Caroline* were acting under the orders of British authorities in Canada, the issue was properly one between the United States government and that of England, not one between Alexander McLeod and the state of New York. Governor William Henry Seward, however, refused to release McLeod, and the division of federal and state powers prevented the Tyler administration from bringing a case involving international relations under its immediate jurisdiction. The consequence was a spectacular federal-state confrontation with important constitutional implications. Webster set forth the dilemma in a letter to Attorney General John J. Crittenden. While the attack upon the *Caroline* raised a question "between independent nations" which should be resolved within the context of international law, Webster wrote on March 15, 1841, the president had no power "to arrest the proceedings" under way in the courts of New York.[12] Despite Webster's firm conviction that the "Constitution of the United States" invested the federal government "with the exclusive control" over "every thing connected with the foreign relations of the Country," Seward proved to be inflexible.[13] Privately characterizing the governor of New York as "a contemptible fellow," Webster planned to seek a writ of error from the U.S. Supreme Court in the event of McLeod's conviction.[14] Ironically, when the case finally went to trial in October 1841, it took the jury less than twenty minutes to declare McLeod, who had an airtight alibi, not guilty. It is a measure of Webster's conservative statesmanship that he used the excitement generated by the McLeod affair to draft a law that empowered U.S. district court and Supreme Court justices to issue writs of habeas corpus when foreign nationals were held for acts committed under the explicit authority of their governments. On August 29, 1842, Congress passed what might be called "the McLeod law."[15] Webster's goal, as he stated in a letter to Senator John M. Berrien, the chairman of the Judiciary Committee, was to safeguard "the peace of the Country," and the new statute made a contribution toward the peaceful resolution of international conflicts.[16]

A third aspect of Webster's conservatism was his inclination, as Richard N. Current wrote, "to think things ought to be kept pretty much as they were."[17] His preference for the status quo expressed itself in the way he approached international relations. While not a pacifist, he tended to view wars as engines of disruption with unpredictable and destabilizing consequences. He opposed territorial expansion by the United States for the same reason. He also had an aversion to aggressive and threatening diplomacy and sought instead the peaceful resolution of international conflicts through compromise. As a freshman congressman from New Hampshire, he spoke out against the War of 1812. When it became clear in 1843 that President Tyler would move toward the annexation of Texas, Webster resigned as secretary of state, both because of his opposition to slavery and concern that it could lead to a war with Mexico. Tyler needed a secretary of state, his son recalled, willing to "go the full length of the Texas question. Certainly that man was not Webster."[18] Reelected to the U.S. Senate from Massachusetts in 1845, he became one of the leading critics of the brinkmanship diplomacy of President James K. Polk. During the debate over the Oregon question in 1846, for example, Webster roundly denounced the president for his "Fifty-four Forty or Fight" rhetoric. "Compromise I can understand—arbitration I can comprehend," the Senator proclaimed, "but negotiation, with a resolution not to settle unless we obtain the whole, is what I do not comprehend in diplomacy on matters of government."[19] Webster was one of fourteen Senators who voted against the Treaty of Guadalupe Hidalgo on March 10, 1848, and he explained why he had done so in a major speech delivered on March 23. He denounced both the war and the treaty as unjust products of land hunger. The conflict with Mexico, he said, was an unconstitutional "war for conquest," and he called for an honorable peace "without territory." He categorically rejected "to-day, and for ever, and to the end, any proposition to add any foreign territory, south or west, north or east, to the States of this Union." Webster believed that the acquisition of California and New Mexico would threaten national unity, and he feared that it might, like the devouring of a large meal by a "rapacious animal," increase the "hunger of dominion" among the American people. There must, the Senator exclaimed, "be some limit to the extent of our territories, and . . . I wished this country should exhibit to the world the example of a powerful republic, without greediness and hunger of empire." It was what Webster called a "plain talk," and it embodied his conservative principles.[20] He valued stability over change, and the best example of this aspect of his conservatism during his service as secretary of state was the Webster-Ashburton Treaty of 1842.

II

Britain and the United States were on a collision course in 1841. McLeod's acquittal on October 12 eased tensions, but that case was but one element in a compound of potentially explosive ingredients which added up to a crisis in Anglo-American relations. The most important problem was the disputed Northeastern boundary between the United States and British North America, which dated to the Peace of Paris of 1783 and involved over 12,000 square miles of land bordering on the four states of Maine, New Hampshire, New York, and Vermont. Also at issue between the two countries was the still unresolved *Caroline* affair; the self-proclaimed right of the British to visit and search American vessels on the high seas in order to suppress the African slave trade; the related and historic quarrel over impressment; the question of renewing the extradition provision of the Jay Treaty, which had expired in 1807; and the *Creole* incident, which occurred after Webster became secretary of state and involved the mutiny of American slaves and their escape to British territory in Nassau, where they were released. All of these issues were on the agenda when Daniel Webster and Lord Ashburton sat down together at the negotiating table in the summer of 1842.

Senator Thomas Hart Benton of Missouri complained that the Webster-Ashburton negotiation had been "tracklessly conducted," and it certainly qualifies as one of the most unusual diplomatic encounters in the history of American foreign policy.[21] Pursuing a plan that he had unsuccessfully recommended to the Van Buren administration in 1839 for an informal approach to the British, Webster studiously avoided protocol and the usual procedures of traditional diplomacy.[22] No minutes were kept and few notes were exchanged. The articles of the treaty and related correspondence dealing with disputes such as the *Caroline* were drafted after Webster and Ashburton had reached agreement and were then submitted to President Tyler for final review. While such personal diplomacy is commonplace in our time, it was unusual by nineteenth-century standards, and it reflected Webster's belief that: "It is only by the exercise of calm reason, that truth can be arrived at, in questions of a complicated nature; and between States, each of which understands and respects the intelligence and power of the other, there ought to be no unwillingness to follow its guidance."[23] In a quiet and relaxed atmosphere, sometimes over a bottle of Madeira wine at Webster's home, the two men calmly dealt with the complex issues that had plagued Anglo-American relations for many years.

Of those issues, the most complicated was the Northeastern boundary, and the two diplomats dealt with in a most atypical fashion. The Webster-Ashburton negotiation was unusual in that it involved four parties, Britain, the United States, and state commissioners from Maine and Massachusetts. Ashburton resented the presence of these quasi-diplomats, but he accepted Webster's argument that their participation was necessary in order to surmount the chief obstacle to a resolution of the Northeastern boundary dispute—the intransigent opposition of Maine to giving up any of the territory that it claimed as its own.[24] In 1838 the legislature of Maine had resolved that it would not accept any proposal by the federal government for a conventional line, and two years later it called upon federal authorities to occupy the area in contention with Britain. The Maine commissioners, as Ashburton observed in 1842, always took "their departure ... from the presumption that the whole Territory belongs to them."[25] In order to overcome the roadblock of state particularism, Webster persuaded the government of Maine to appoint commissioners authorized to consent to a compromise of the boundary issue. Although the presence of the contentious men of Maine nearly destroyed the entire negotiation and compelled Webster to play the role of mediator between them and the British envoy, in the end it produced a settlement that circumvented complex constitutional and political dilemmas and satisfied the honor and interests of all the parties.

With a touch of vanity, Webster later wrote that the "grand stroke" which nobody had even thought of before but which led to "the fortunate result of the whole negotiation" was the hazardous inclusion of representatives of Maine and Massachusetts in the negotiating process.[26]

In a senior composition written at Dartmouth College in 1801 on the question whether deception is ever justifiable, Webster answered in the affirmative. There "are cases," he stated, "in which the good to be obtained is far greater than the evil resulting from the use of means, otherwise wrong. So deception, though commonly not justifiable, sometimes produces so much good, that we are warranted in the use of it."[27] In 1842 the end sought was a stable relationship with Great Britain, and Webster did not hesitate to use Machiavellian means, which constitutes another rather unusual aspect of the Webster-Ashburton negotiations. In order to moderate the behavior of the inhabitants of Maine, Webster adopted a plan set forth by Francis O. J. Smith, a newspaper publisher and former Democratic congressman from that state.[28] The idea was to induce the people, politicians, and press of Maine to agree to the appointment of state commissioners authorized to participate in and to consent to a negotiated compromise of the disputed northeastern boundary. To accomplish this end, Smith and Webster carried out a ten-month sub rosa propaganda campaign financed out of the secret service fund. Although that account had been established by Congress in 1810 "for the contingent expenses of intercourse between the United States and foreign nations," Webster drew $12,000 from it to plant articles in journals and newspapers, to circulate pacific memorials, and to pay lobbyists such as Professor Jared Sparks of Harvard College.[29] Sparks, for example, made a special trip to Augusta in May, 1842, to show Governor John Fairfield two maps, one drawn by Sparks himself, indicating that cartographical evidence tended to support the British boundary claim. Webster himself undertook a similar mission to Massachusetts, and he also authored unsigned editorials in the *National Intelligencer*, one of the most influential newspapers of the day, emphasizing the theme that a negotiated settlement was the only alternative to a calamitous war.[30] Webster also sent the famous Sparks map, along with the finished treaty and other documents, to the U.S. Senate, the implication being that if that body failed to consent to the agreement, the cartographical evidence would work to the disadvantage of the United States in the event of a future arbitration of the boundary dispute. The well orchestrated Smith-Webster campaign culminated in the votes of the Maine legislature on May 26 to appoint commissioners empowered to accept a conventional line and of the U.S. Senate on August 20 to approve the Treaty of Washington by the surprisingly large margin of 39 to 9. Richard N. Current has pointed out that the Webster-Ashburton accord was as much a triumph in "the manipulation of public opinion" as it was an achievement of diplomacy, and Frederick Merk has criticized Webster for undermining the principles of federal-state relations and violating the law of 1810 by subsidizing "underground electioneering to manage the sentiment of a state of the Union."[31] As Merk conceded, however, the Treaty of Washington did have the merit "of preserving peace."[32]

While some of the means employed were improper, the ends achieved were impressive. Ashburton and Webster devised what Attorney General Hugh S. Legaré characterized as a "chef d'oeuvre" of diplomacy.[33] The Treaty of Washington resolved boundary disputes as old as the Republic itself and brought tranquillity to a Canadian-American frontier that had been troubled since 1837. Article 8 of the agreement, the joint cruising convention, in which both countries promised to maintain an independent naval force of at least eighty guns off the west coast of Africa to cooperate in suppressing the slave trade, quieted the visit and search controversy. The extradition article helped put an end to the lawless operations of such groups as the Patriot Hunters, a secret society of Canadian rebels and American sympathizers, and it served as a model for extradition agreements with other countries. Both the *Caroline* and *Creole* disputes were finessed in supplemental correspondence accompanying the treaty which had the merit of allowing these issues to be forgotten. Webster's famous letter on impressment of August 8, 1842, did not settle that intractible problem, but it facilitated American acceptance of the accord by appealing to national pride. In terms of consequences, the Treaty of Washington ended a potentially explosive crisis in Anglo-American relations, fixed the boundary that now exists between Canada and the United States, left little of a significant nature other than the Oregon question for the United States and Britain to quarrel over, and paved the way for a rapprochement between the two English-speaking nations.[34] Above all, as Webster emphasized in 1846 in a two-day speech defending the treaty before the Senate, it had advanced the cause of world peace.[35]

In several respects, the Treaty of Washington embodies Webster's conservative statesmanship. As suggested in a heated debate that he carried on in 1842–1843 with Lewis Cass, an Anglophobe who resigned as U.S. minister to France in protest over Article 8, the treaty remained within the parameters of the maxims of George Washington.[36] On November 14, 1842, Webster ridiculed Cass's critique as a "tissue of mistakes" and maintained that the United States had not "departed in this treaty, in the slightest degree, from their former principles of avoiding European combinations upon subjects not American," and pointed out that the United States itself had taken "the first great steps" against the slave trade by declaring it to be piracy in 1820.[37] Webster's preference for stability was written into almost every stipulation of the accord, and it is worth mentioning that the Treaty of Washington is the only international agreement in American history in which the United States relinquished a substantial amount of territory that it claimed as its own. Unlike most of his predecessors and successors in the office of secretary of state, Webster did not believe that a few hundred square miles of land outweighed a stable relationship with America's most important trading partner and source of financial credit. The agreement with Ashburton illustrates as well Webster's conviction that diplomacy should be the handmaiden of commerce, another aspect of his conservative philosophy of foreign affairs.

III

The best example of Webster's commercial orientation was the pioneering role he played in the establishment of an American foreign policy toward East Asia and the Pacific region. During his first incumbency in the Department of State, he authored the so-called Tyler Doctrine of December 30, 1842, which defined the Hawaiian islands as an American sphere of influence. Of equal importance, he wrote the instruction of May 8, 1843, which set forth the guidelines for Caleb Cushing's mission to China. During the second term as secretary of state, Webster forcefully reiterated the Tyler Doctrine and drafted the original directive of June 10, 1851, to John H. Aulick for what eventually became the Perry mission to Japan. When Webster took office in 1841, the United States was not a Pacific power and had not devised a systematic approach toward that part of the world. By 1852, however, the United States had fashioned a discriminating policy of commercial expansion for East Asia and the Pacific, and, more than any other single individual, Webster was at the center of that development. The initiatives toward Hawaii, China, and Japan were all undertaken to promote and protect commercial interests, and they reflected certain inclinations and predispositions acquired by Webster during a long career in law and politics.

"The commercial world," Charles M. Wiltse has written, "with its robust subsidiaries, manufacturing, banking, and transportation, had constituted the setting for Webster's professional life since his admission to the Massachusetts bar in 1805."[38] Importers like Charles March, China merchants like Thomas Handasyd Perkins, bankers like Nicholas Biddle, and manufacturers like Abbott Lawrence were his clients, his friends, and his constituents. As a lawyer-politician, he ably represented their interests from 1805 until his death. As a life-long New Englander, moreover, he came from that section of the country that was most closely related to the international economy. New England, Paul A. Varg wrote, "was as tied to the sea as the western pioneer was tied to the soil."[39] To the merchants and manufacturers of the Northeast, disruptions in foreign markets meant financial hardship. They preferred peace and commerce to international instability and territorial expansion, and so did Webster.[40] To them, and to Webster, the great chain that united all the nations of the world was navigation and commerce, and government had a responsibility to protect and promote those vital interests.

In Hawaii, the problem was possible domination of that strategically-located but fragile kingdom by the French. Since the early nineteenth century, the Hawaiian islands had served as a way station in the China trade and as the center of a thriving American whaling industry in the Pacific. By the 1840s, primarily as a result of the activities of New England merchants and missionaries, Americans had come to dominate the economic and cultural life of the islands. Beginning in 1839, however, because of commercial and religious discrimination by the Hawaiian government against their nationals, the French used gunboat diplomacy to extract concessions from King Kamehameha III, thereby exposing the weakness of his kingdom and raising the spectre that Hawaii might come under the control of a European power.[41] In December, 1842, William Richards and Timoteo Haalilio arrived in Washington as special envoys from Kamehameha. Their purpose was to preserve Hawaiian territorial integrity by securing international recognition of the independence of the islands. Richards, a Protestant American missionary who had become one of the most important counselors to Kamehameha, elicited a response from the Tyler administration by hinting that if the United States did not support Hawaiian sovereignty Britain might be asked to establish a protectorate over the islands.[42]

President Tyler set forth the doctrine that bears his name in a special message to Congress of December 30, 1842. In words drafted by Webster, the president began by pointing out that the Hawaiian islands were closer to North America than to any other continent, that they were especially important to the American whale fishery in the Pacific Ocean, that American citizens held substantial property investments in the islands, and that five-sixths of all the vessels visiting them annually were American. For these reasons, the United States government would be dissatisfied "at any attempt by another power . . . to take possession of the islands, colonize them, and subvert the native Government." Any nation impinging upon Hawaiian sovereignty could anticipate "a decided remonstrance" from the United States.[43] With this declaration, the Tyler administration stated its intention to support Hawaiian independence because of the preponderance of American economic interests there, extended the noncolonization and nonintervention principles of the Monroe Doctrine to Hawaii, and established a foreign policy toward Hawaii that lasted until the United States annexed the islands in 1898. In 1842, however, colonialism was unequivocally repudiated. Tyler disclaimed any desire to acquire special commercial advantages or control over the Hawaiian kingdom. Rather, the goals sought were equality of commercial access and the maintenance of the territorial integrity of a weak nation threatened by European domination.[44] When Lord Aberdeen, the British foreign secretary, assessed the Tyler Doctrine as a ploy to establish an American protectorate over the Hawaiian islands, Webster responded by disclaiming a "sinister purpose" of any kind. America's course toward Hawaii, he emphasized, was a "conservative" one of not seeking any exclusive privileges and of upholding "the independence of those Islands."[45]

The foreign policy fashioned by the Tyler administration for China was also anchored upon a commercially-oriented assessment of the nature of American national interests. With respect to China, the perceived threat was possible economic advantage by the British. The Treaty of Nanking of August 29, 1842, which ended the Opium War, provided for the opening of four new ports to British traders and for the establishment of regular commercial duties. Whether the United States would share in the benefits gained by the British was an open question. In the same message in which he set forth the Tyler Doctrine, the president, again using words drafted by his secretary of state, asked Congress for funds to send a commissioner to China. The rationale for the request was solely economic. After pointing out that the Nanking agreement did not provide for the admission of ships of nations other than England and mentioning that American trade continued to be restricted to "the single port of Canton," Tyler observed that because of the "mercantile interest of the United States" it was important to gain equal access to the new treaty ports of Amoy, Foochow, Ningpo, and Shanghai. He anticipated, moreover, an increased Chinese demand for Western goods and optimistically looked forward to an enhanced commercial relationship with an "Empire supposed to contain 300,000,000 subjects, fertile in various rich products of the earth."[46]

On March 3, 1843, Congress appropriated $40,000 to send an envoy to China, and a few days later Webster told his friend, Thomas B. Curtis, that he considered the China mission to be more significant than any that had "ever proceeded from this Country, & more important than any other, likely to succeed it, in our days."[47] Webster's actions matched his words, and he devoted much attention to formulating the instructions that were to guide Caleb Cushing. On March 20, Webster issued a circular asking "intelligent persons" familiar with China to provide the Department of State with advice about how to cultivate friendly relations with that nation and how to enlarge "commercial intercourse between the two countries."[48] The half dozen responses were all from merchants interested in the China trade, most of whom were known personally to the secretary of state, and their suggestions had a discernible impact upon Webster's thinking.[49]

Like the American merchants engaged in the China trade, Webster emphasized in the instruction to Cushing of May 8, 1843, that the primary goal was to "secure the entry of American ships and cargoes" into the treaty ports "on terms as favorable as those which are enjoyed by English merchants." Cushing was to tell the Chinese that American friendship depended upon the negotiation of an agreement that provided for most-favored-nation status for Americans in the China market.[50] In contrast to the protective nature of the Tyler Doctrine, the China mission was designed to enlarge American commercial interests. Cushing achieved that end in 1844 when he signed the Treaty of Wanghia, which established diplomatic relations between the United States and China and placed American trading rights on a legal basis comparable to that obtained by the British. Webster's instruction of May 8, 1843, which guided Cushing's diplomacy, contained the first comprehensive statement of American policy toward China and formed the basis of that policy until superseded by the Open Door Notes of 1899–1900, of which it was the godfather. Along with the Tyler Doctrine, the China instruction constitutes one of Webster's outstanding diplomatic legacies, and they share an important similarity. With respect to both China and Hawaii, Webster sought equality of commercial access to markets that were in danger of coming under the dominance of one of the great powers of Europe. The China instruction also constituted Webster's last official act as Tyler's secretary of state. On the same day that he initialed the directive to Cushing, Webster signed his letter of resignation.

During Webster's second tenure as secretary of state, Hawaii became an object of great concern. Once again, the problem was a French threat of intervention. The situation was complicated by a prospective annexation of Hawaii to the United States. On March 10, 1851, Kamehameha III, anticipating the use of military force by the French, gave Luther Severance, the U.S. commissioner, a secret document transferring his sovereignty over the Hawaiian kingdom to the United States in the event of an outbreak of hostilities with France.[51] Severance assured the king of American military support and recommended to Webster that the United States annex the islands. "We must not take the islands in virtue of the 'manifest destiny' principle," he wrote Webster on March 18, "but can we not accept their voluntary offer?"[52]

In formulating a policy response, Webster acted in accordance with his conservative principles. On July 14, 1851, he sent two remarkable communications to Severance. The first letter, in the form of an official instruction which was to be shown to the French, contained a vigorous reaffirmation of the Tyler Doctrine. After pointing out that the Hawaiian islands were even more important economically to the United States than they had been in 1842, Webster made it clear that the Fillmore administration would not allow them to be possessed by any of "the great commercial powers of Europe." The U.S. Navy, he concluded, would be directed to maintain sufficient armament in the Pacific Ocean to preserve "the honor and dignity of the United States and the safety of the Government of the Hawaiian Islands."[53]

Knowing that the directive of July 14 would be received by an American commissioner whose "head is full of dangerous ideas,"

Webster also sent Severance a carefully-worded letter of private instructions.[54] In considerable detail, the secretary of state explained the war power to the former congressman from Maine. Since the Constitution vested the war-initiating prerogative "entirely with Congress," Severance was not to "direct, request, or encourage" any American naval officer to commit hostilities against the French. With respect to the "very important question" of annexation, Webster ordered Severance to return the document transferring Hawaiian sovereignty to the United States. The American commissioner was authorized only to indicate the strong commitment of the United States to maintaining Hawaiian independence. All other matters had to be decided in Washington.[55] Severance complied fully with Webster's stringent instructions, and the danger passed when the French refrained from the use of military force.

If the Hawaiian crisis of 1851 can be viewed as a test case of consistency, Webster passed the examination with flying colors. He did not deviate from the principles of 1842, and he adhered to his constitutional and anti-territorial expansionist convictions. Webster also acted from a belief that an open door for American commerce in Hawaii was even more important to the United States in the 1850s than it had been in the 1840s. As President Millard Fillmore stated in his second annual message to Congress on December 2, 1851, the significance of the Hawaiian islands to the United States had been "greatly enhanced" because of the acquisition of California and Oregon. They were immediately valuable "as a place of refuge and refreshment for our vessels engaged in the whale fishery" and prospectively valuable "by the consideration that they lie in the course of that great trade which must at no distant day be carried on between the western coast of North America and eastern Asia."[56]

At the same time that Fillmore and Webster were defending American interests in Hawaii, they were also planning a naval expedition to Japan. Except for a strictly regulated trade with the Dutch at the tiny island of Deshima and some commerce with the Chinese, Japan had been closed to the world since 1638. Webster was resolved to change that situation for reasons that he set forth in two key documents dated May 10 and June 10, 1851. On May 10 Webster completed and countersigned a letter from President Fillmore to the emperor of Japan. The Japanese were asked to help American vessels wrecked upon their coasts, to allow Americans to engage in trade, and to provide a place where steamers going from California to China could purchase a portion of their supposedly abundant supply of coal. "Our object," the letter emphasized, "is friendly commercial intercourse, and nothing more."[57] While similar in content and tone, the June 10 instruction to John H. Aulick, the commander of the East India Squadron, more clearly revealed the administration's purposes. While it was "important" to secure the right to trade at Japanese ports and "even more important" to obtain a Japanese promise to protect shipwrecked American seamen and vessels, the main object of the mission was to persuade the Japanese to sell Americans "that great necessary of commerce," coal.[58]

Webster possessed a keen interest in such new technologies as oceanic steam navigation, and he believed that the future of international commerce lay with the steamship. The already profitable China trade had grown substantially after the negotiation of the Treaty of Wanghia in 1844, but securing adequate and accessible supplies of coal presented a problem.[59] Not only did the crude marine engines of the day burn large quantities of the fuel, thereby taking up valuable cargo space, but also the coal had to be supplied by colliers from Britain or the Atlantic ports of the United States. The Japanese islands, however, lay directly in the path of the so-called great circle route between San Francisco and Shanghai and were rumored to possess ample deposits of coal.[60] Japan, Aulick was told, was a "link in the chain of oceanic steam-navigation," and his mission was to take the steps necessary "to enable our enterprising merchants to supply the last link in that great chain, which unites all nations of the world, by the early establishment of a line of steamers from California to China."[61]

Recalled in November 1851 to face charges of misconduct, Aulick never had the opportunity to try his hand at implementing Webster's directive, and Webster himself died before Matthew C. Perry set sail for Japan. Nevertheless, the Perry expedition was the "last link" in a "great chain" that had in large measure been forged by the statesman from Massachusetts. The thread that tied Hawaii, China, and Japan together was Webster's assumption that the federal government had a responsibility to protect and enlarge the commercial interests of its citizens. He was an optimistic commercial expansionist who possessed a global maritime view. At a dinner in Boston in 1851 celebrating the victory of the schooner *America* in the yacht race at Cowes, Webster paid a warm tribute to the ingenuity of Americans, "who may soon command the ocean, both oceans, all oceans."[62] There was, however, no threat of colonialism in Webster's rhetoric or in his strategy of commercial expansion. He looked upon trade as a civilizing force that promoted international stability and mutual understanding among nations, and he disavowed any special economic privileges or territorial ambitions for the United States. The goals he sought were unhindered access to the markets of East Asia and the Pacific islands on a most-favored-nation basis and maintaining the territorial integrity and political neutrality of weak states like Hawaii.

IV

As suggested by Webster's strategy of commercial expansion for the Pacific and East Asia, he was a calculating nationalist. Since the famous debate with Senator Robert Y. Hayne in 1830, he had earned a well deserved reputation as the outstanding spokesman for American nationalism. Webster was no parochial chauvinist, once commenting to the French minister to the United States that American institutions were "peculiar & what suits us may not . . . be suitable" to others, but he was an ardent patriot.[63] Nationalism, tempered by a degree of cosmopolitanism, constitutes the central element in Webster's conservative philosophy.

While many examples could be chosen to illustrate the nationalist aspect of Webster's conservative approach to international relations, perhaps the best is the so-called Hülsemann Letter of December 21, 1850. The republic was in peril in 1850, not by threat from without but by dissension from within over the slavery question. Webster's main objective in accepting the post of secretary of state for a second time was not to bring his expertise to bear on issues of international policy, but rather to contribute to internal solidarity by furthering acceptance of the Compromise of 1850. When the Austrian chargé d'affaires to the United States gave Webster an unusual opportunity to use foreign policy to promote national unity, he did not hesitate to seize the moment. Although Webster had tried to persuade the Chevalier Johann Georg Hülsemann not to make a long delayed protest against the previous administration's support for the Hungarian revolution, the brash and punctilious Austrian issued a blistering remonstrance on September 30, 1850. Hülsemann's disdainful note was characterized by such indelicacies as referring curtly to American ignorance of European affairs and describing an American diplomat as a "spy."[64] It was, as William Hunter, a clerk in the Department of State commented, "sufficiently arrogant and saucy to justify us in requiring him to take it back." Hunter advised against such a course, however. Instead, he suggested making a reply "to tell to . . . advantage on the public ear and to the public mind."[65] Hunter's recommendation was immediately adopted by a secretary of state far more troubled by the condition of the Union than by the status of Austrian-American relations.

On December 21, Webster replied to Hülsemann with what has been characterized aptly as a lengthy "hymn of praise to American institutions, achievements, and destiny."[66] He boastfully contrasted the power and extent of the Austrian empire with that of the American republic, "in comparison with which the possessions of the house of Hapsburg are but a patch on the earth's surface." Had an American diplomat been treated as a spy, he warned sternly, the American people "would have demanded immediate hostilities" waged to the utmost against Austria. Webster also expressed indifference toward any possible acts of retaliation Austria might conceivably undertake against the United States, and, in a tone more appropriate to a Fourth of July oration than to a state paper, proclaimed that "nothing will deter either the government or the people of the United States from exercising, at their own discretion, the rights belonging to them as an independent nation."[67]

Scholars have been uniformly critical of Webster's letter, calling it, among other epithets, a "play to the gallery," a brash and gratuitous lecture," and a "preposterous note." The essence of the critique is that the secretary of state had committed a grave and irresponsible indiscretion in giving in to the temptation to use a foreign policy issue to promote domestic political ends.[68] Although the charge is well founded, in a sense it misses the point. There is little doubt that the letter to Hülsemann was aimed more at the American people than at the international community. In the fall of 1850 there was considerable opposition to the Compromise from both Northerners and Southerners, and Webster's consuming preoccupation was "to preserve the Institutions of our Fathers."[69] Webster, then, had used foreign policy to promote internal unity, but he had not acted irresponsibly.

Despite an outpouring of public and private enthusiasm over the Hülsemann Letter, Webster did not seek to exploit further his advantage over Hülsemann. On the contrary, since he had no desire to impair seriously Austrian-American relations over issues he had originally conceived of as unimportant in themselves, Webster acquiesced in an exchange of notes by means of which the two diplomats had terminated amicably the correspondence on the subject by March 1851. As Edward Everett recalled, the letter did not produce even "a temporary suspension of friendly relations between the United States and Austria."[70] There was, moreover, no danger of armed conflict with Austria, and Webster had only risked breaking diplomatic relations with a country of peripheral concern to the United States. Trade with Austria was slight, and it is even doubtful whether the two countries could have found a place in which to fight one another had they wanted to, which they did not. Webster, in sum, had measured the possible costs in playing politics with American foreign policy. He perceived the domestic crisis over slavery to be of such magnitude as to supercede the possibility of jeopardizing relations with Austria, and the United States may have gained more than it lost from Webster's manipulation of the politics of foreign policy. In a letter written to G. A. Tavenner six months before his death, Webster stated that "nothing but a deep sense of duty" had led him to take the part he did in bringing about the Compromise of 1850, and, he continued, "that same sense of duty" remained "with unabated force."[71] The harm done Austrian-American relations by the Hülsemann Letter was negligible; Webster had not acted out of impulse; and he was proud to have "rendered the Country some service."[72]

In terms of Webster's overall service as secretary of state from 1841 to 1843 and 1850 to 1852, the flag-waving bombast of the Hülsemann Letter was atypical. His state papers usually were models of decorum and tightly-reasoned logic, and he generally conducted the foreign policy of the United States in a prudent and moderate fashion. Courtly and dignified in bearing, even his personal mannerisms were conservative. Webster was not always consistent, as suggested by a quixotic attempt to seize the Lobos islands from Peru in 1852, and he could be Machiavellian, as suggested by the means employed to gain approval of the Treaty of Washington.[73] He also was not above using foreign policy for domestic purposes, as suggested by the Hülsemann episode. His hope, as he put it on the occasion of his resignation as secretary of state in 1843, was to leave office with the country in "as good condition" as he had found it.[74] Through the theory and practice of conservative statesmanship, he did indeed achieve that goal.

NOTES

1. Alexander De Conde, *The American Secretary of State: An Interpretation* (New York, 1962), p. 172; David L. Porter, "The Ten Best

147

Secretaries of State—And the Five Worst," *American Heritage,* 33 (December 1981), pp. 78-80.

2. Daniel Webster to Edward Everett, May 6, 1851, in Fletcher Webster, ed., *The Private Correspondence of Daniel Webster* (2 vols.; Boston, 1857), II, 442.

3. James W. McIntyre, ed., *The Writings and Speeches of Daniel Webster* (18 vols.; New York, 1903), XII, 181-86; hereafter cited *Writings and Speeches.*

4. Webster to John F. Crampton, April 29, 1852, National Archives, Record Group 59, Notes to Foreign Legations, Britain.

5. Webster to Robert Blair Campbell, January 14, 1843, in Kenneth E. Shewmaker, Kenneth R. Stevens, and Anita McGurn, eds., *The Papers of Daniel Webster, Diplomatic Papers, Volume 1, 1841-1843* (Hanover, N.H., and London, England, 1983), pp. 369-72; hereafter cited *Diplomatic Papers of Webster.*

6. Edward Everett, ed., *The Works of Daniel Webster* (6 vols.; Boston, 1851), III, 200.

7. For the Tyler Doctrine see *Diplomatic Papers of Webster,* pp. 851-77.

8. Webster to Fox, April 24, 1841, in *Diplomatic Papers of Webster,* pp. 58-68.

9. Verbatim record of the 1939th meeting of the United Nations Security Council, July 9, 1976; Verbatim record of the 2282nd meeting of the United Nations Security Council, June 15, 1981.

10. Charles Francis Adams, ed., *Memoirs of John Quincy Adams* (12 vols.; Philadelphia, 1874-1877), XI, 36.

11. Palmerston to Fox, February 9, 1841, FO 97/19, Public Record Office, London, England.

12. Webster to Crittenden, March 15, 1841, in *Diplomatic Papers of Webster,* pp. 45-48.

13. Webster to Joshua A. Spencer, September 21, 1841, in *ibid.,* p. 146.

14. Webster to Hiram Ketchum, [July 1841], in *ibid.,* pp. 99-100.

15. See 5 *U.S. Stat.* 539-40.

16. Webster to Berrien, January 14, 1842, in *Diplomatic Papers of Webster,* pp. 707-08.

17. Richard N. Current, *Daniel Webster and the Rise of National Conservatism* (Boston and Toronto, 1955), p. 10.

18. Lyon G. Tyler, ed., *The Letters and Times of the Tylers* (3 vols.; Richmond and Williamsburg, 1884-1896), II, 263-64.

19. Remarks of February 26, 1846, in *Congressional Globe,* 29th Cong., 1st sess., p. 432.

20. Edwin P. Whipple, ed., *The Great Speeches and Orations of Daniel Webster* (Boston, 1884), pp. 551-68.

21. *Congressional Globe,* 27th Cong., 3rd sess., app., p. 14.

22. See "Memorandum on the Northeast Boundary Negotiations" in *The Papers of Daniel Webster, Correspondence* (7 vols.; Hanover, N.H.,

and London, England, 1974-198-), IV, 346-49; hereafter cited *Correspondence of Webster*.

23. Webster to Everett, January 29, 1842, in *Diplomatic Papers of Webster*, p. 177.
24. See Ashburton to Webster, July 1, 1842, in *ibid.*, p. 604.
25. Ashburton to Webster, c. July 2, 1842, in *ibid.*, pp. 604-05.
26. Webster to Jared Sparks, March 11, 1843, in *ibid.*, pp. 785-87.
27. Senior composition of May 4, 1801, in *Correspondence of Webster*, I, 32.
28. See Smith to Webster, [June 7, 1841], in *Diplomatic Papers of Webster*, pp. 94-96.
29. 2 *U.S. Stat.* 608-09.
30. See, for example, "Editorial: The Treaty of Washington," August 22, 1842, in *Diplomatic Papers of Webster*, pp. 693-95.
31. Current, "Webster's Propaganda and the Ashburton Treaty," *Mississippi Valley Historical Review*, 34 (September 1947), p. 187; Merk, *Fruits of Propaganda in the Tyler Administration* (Cambridge, Mass., 1971), pp. 72, 89.
32. Merk, *Fruits of Propaganda*, p. 32.
33. Legaré to Webster, July 29, 1842, in *Diplomatic Papers of Webster*, pp. 656-57.
34. For the best account of the Webster-Ashburton negotiations and treaty see Howard Jones, *To the Webster-Ashburton Treaty: A Study in Anglo-American Relations, 1783-1843* (Chapel Hill, 1977).
35. "Defence of the Treaty of Washington," in *Writings and Speeches*, IX, 78-150.
36. For the Cass-Webster debate, see *Diplomatic Papers of Webster*, pp. 710-75.
37. Webster to Cass, November 14, 1842, in *ibid.*, pp. 724-34.
38. Wiltse, "Foreward," in *ibid.*
39. Varg, *New England and Foreign Relations 1789-1850* (Hanover, N.H., and London, England, 1983), p. 3.
40. *Ibid.*, p. 215.
41. For the background to the Tyler Doctrine see Ralph S. Kuykendall, *The Hawaiian Kingdom 1778-1854: Foundation and Transformation* (Honolulu, 1938), and Harold Whitman Bradley, *The American Frontier in Hawaii: The Pioneers, 1789-1843* (Stanford, California, 1942).
42. The Journal of William Richards, December 29, 1842, cited in Bradley, *op. cit.*, pp. 443-44.
43. James D. Richardson, ed., *A Compilation of the Messages and Papers of the Presidents, 1789-1897* (10 vols.; Washington, D.C., 1896-1899), IV, 211-12; hereafter cited *Messages and Papers*.
44. *Ibid.*
45. Webster to Everett, March 23, 1843, in *Diplomatic Papers of Webster*, p. 876.

46. *Messages and Papers*, IV, 211-14.
47. Webster to Curtis, March 12, 1843, in *Diplomatic Papers of Webster*, pp. 899-901.
48. Department of State circular, March 20, 1843 in *ibid.*, pp. 901-02.
49. For the responses to the circular of March 20, 1843, see *ibid.*, pp. 903-21.
50. Webster to Cushing, May 8, 1843, in *ibid.*, pp. 922-26.
51. Kamehameha III, March 10, 1851, in *Senate Executive Documents*, 52nd Cong., 2nd sess., No. 77, pp. 84-85.
52. Severance to Webster, March 18, 1851, National Archives, Record Group 59, Despatches From U.S. Ministers, Hawaii.
53. No. 4. Webster to Severance, July 14, 1851, National Archives, Record Group 59, Diplomatic and Consular Instructions, Hawaii.
54. Webster to Millard Fillmore, July 21, 1851, Fillmore Papers, Buffalo and Erie County Historical Society.
55. Webster to Severance, July 14, 1851, National Archives, Record Group 59, Diplomatic and Consular Instructions, Hawaii.
56. *Messages and Papers*, V, 120.
57. Fillmore to the Emperor of Japan, May 10, 1851, National Archives, Record Group 59, Communications to Foreign Sovereigns and Heads of State.
58. Webster to Aulick, June 10, 1851, National Archives, Record Group 59, Special Missions.
59. For the growth of the China trade see Eldon Griffin, *Clippers and Consuls: American Consular and Commercial Relations with Eastern Asia, 1845-1860* (Ann Arbor, Michigan, 1938), pp. 308-309.
60. John W. Oliver, *History of American Technology* (New York, 1956), pp. 199-202; Robert J. Rayback, *Millard Fillmore: Biography of a President* (Buffalo, 1959), p. 312.
61. Webster to Aulick, June 10, 1851.
62. Cited in Oliver, *History of American Technology*, p. 261.
63. Webster to Eugène de Sartiges, February 6, 1852, Webster Papers, New Hampshire Historical Society.
64. Hülsemann to Webster, September 30, 1850, National Archives, Record Group 59, Notes From Foreign Legations, Austria.
65. Hunter to Webster, October 4, 1850, Webster Papers, New Hampshire Historical Society.
66. Robert F. Dalzell, *Daniel Webster and the Trial of American Nationalism, 1843-1852* (Boston, 1973), p. 226.
67. *Writings and Speeches*, XII, 165-178.
68. Samuel Flagg Bemis, *A Diplomatic History of the United States* (New York, 1936), p. 311; Robert H. Ferrell, *American Diplomacy: A History* (New York, 1969), pp. 250-251; Robert A. Brent, "Tarnished Brass: A New Perspective on Daniel Webster," *Southern Quarterly*, 4 (October 1965), pp. 49-50; Graham H. Stuart, *The Department of*

State: A History of Its Organization, Procedure, and Personnel (New York, 1949), pp. 114-115.

69. Webster to William Prescott, November 7, 1850, Webster Papers, New Hampshire Historical Society.
70. Everett [ed.], *The Original Draft of the Hülsemann Letter* (Boston, 1853), p. v.
71. Webster to Tavenner, April 9, 1852, Webster Papers, New Hampshire Historical Society.
72. Webster to Cameron F. McRies, July 10, 1851, Webster Papers, Dartmouth College.
73. For the Lobos islands episode see Shewmaker, " 'Untaught Diplomacy': Daniel Webster and the Lobos Islands Controversy," *Diplomatic History,* 1 (Fall 1977), pp. 321-340.
74. Webster to Thomas B. Curtis, April 29, 1843, in *Diplomatic Papers of Webster,* p. 931.

7

WILLIAM H. SEWARD
AND THE FAITH OF A NATION

Norman B. Ferris

William Henry Seward, born in 1801, served as secretary of state from 1861 to 1869. Most diplomatic historians agree that he had few peers in conducting this country's foreign relations.[1] During the American Civil War his diplomacy, designed to prevent the introduction of European power into the conflict, was conducted, according to one authority, "with astonishing effectiveness." The leading European powers, after initially issuing proclamations granting belligerent status to the Confederacy, never took the second and final, threatening step to full diplomatic recognition. They had good reasons for avoiding that decision, but Seward's determined efforts to remind them of that fact contributed immeasurably to the success of the Union cause.[2] After the Civil War Seward continued as an active and largely successful secretary of state, drawing on the wisdom he had accumulated during a long public career.[3]

Seward's model statesman was John Quincy Adams. The New Yorker admired the sixth president chiefly because, as he declared in his eulogy delivered in 1848 following the death of his political exemplar, Adams believed "that the tenure of human power is on condition of its being beneficently exercised for the common welfare of the human race." Adams, said Seward, had sought unselfishly to serve not only his own country but also the cause of human kind. Throughout his adult life Seward endeavored to remain faithful to this great ideal of service which he attributed to

Adams. His actions as a public man, including those as American secretary of state, can be fully understood in no other context.[4] Seward, like Adams, understood the nation's ideals, but he also recognized its interests and pursued them with a remarkable grasp of the power available to him and to others.

As he advanced in politics during the 1830s from state senator and party spokesman in the New York legislature to become the first Whig governor of that state, Seward, no less than his predecessors, sustained a reverence for the doctrine of universal human rights. Since the dawn of recorded history, he believed, mankind had lived "under monarchical and aristocratic systems of government," which ruled through oppression, depredation, and slavery. Society had always been "divided into classes—the rich and the poor, the strong and the dependent, the learned and the unlearned—and from this inequality of social condition . . . resulted the ignorance, the crime, and the sufferings of the people."[5] The Federal Union, Seward continued, was born "to bring all mankind from a state of servitude to the exercise of self-government—from under the tyranny of physical force to the gentle sway of opinion—from under subjection to matter to domination over nature." It was the task of Americans "to lead the way, to take up the cross of republicanism and bear it before the nations," remembering always that the American democratic system was "founded in the natural equality of *all* men—not alone all *American* men, nor alone all *white* men, but all men of every country, clime, and complexion, . . . not made equal by human laws, but born equal."[6]

Seward viewed the United States as a nation of destiny in human affairs. For him the Constitution was a document designed "not merely . . . to secure the 'largest liberty to the greatest number of our citizens,' but as the means of extending throughout the world the knowledge of the inalienable rights of man to self-government, and of the means by which that inestimable right may be established and secured." America's twenty millions, declared Seward, "are expanding to two hundred millions—our originally narrow domain into a great empire. Its destiny is to renovate the condition of mankind." It would accomplish this by furnishing an "example . . . which cannot but have the most favorable influence on mankind." The American Union would be "the last and fairest experiment of human nature." It was the "ark of safety in which are deposited the hopes of the world." Its mission, "so noble and so benevolent," required "a generous and self-denying

154

enthusiasm, . . . beneficence without ambition."[7]

Seward's vision of an expanding American influence in the affairs of mankind, like that of John Quincy Adams, did not contemplate the use of force. Rather it was anchored, like the sense of mission shared by his predecessors—Jefferson, Madison, Clay, Webster—to the assumption that the United States, demonstrating the capacity of a free people to govern themselves with intelligence, would comprise a model which other peoples would seek to emulate. "[The] extension and perfection of institutions similar to our own throughout the world," he declared, was "not to be obtained suddenly, by enthusiasm or by violence," but rather "by long and persevering efforts; and the efforts which are most successful are such as tend most to improve ourselves, and to produce harmony and peace among our fellow-men." Thus Seward was never bellicose in expressing his sense of mission, limiting it to the recommendation of republican institutions to other nations. His policy was to "expand not by force of arms, but by attraction." To accomplish this the American government should be "moderate and pacific, yet always frank, decided and firm, in bearing its testimony against error and oppression; and while abstaining from forcible intervention in foreign disputes, yet always fearlessly rendering to the cause of republicanism everywhere, by influence and example, all the aid that the laws of nations do not peremptorily, or, in their true spirit, forbid."[8]

Seward looked with pleasure on the independence of Latin America and its halting progress toward republican government. He was fond of reminding his countrymen that when the "ever-advancing American Revolution" had reached the Spanish and Portuguese colonies in the New World and spawned "seven new republics, with constitutions differing not widely from our own," Spain had "appealed to the Holy League of Europe for their aid, and the new republics appealed to the United States for that recognition which could not fail to impart strength." John Quincy Adams, as secretary of state, had believed "the emancipation of Spanish America was necessary for our own larger freedom and . . . security." Adams had obtained from Congress the recognition of the independence of the Latin American republics and then, to give decisive effect to that decision, President Monroe had "solemnly declared to the world that thenceforth any attempt by any foreign power" to reinstate colonialism in the Western Hemisphere would be opposed by the United States.[9]

Seward, like Adams, harbored a distrust of Europe. Europe, he feared, remained antagonistic to the forms of government existing in the New World. But its despots, he warned, trying instinctively to suppress the liberalizing and equalizing forces that had arisen in the West, might inadvertently rouse sleeping aspirations and ambitions in their own subjects. Thus for the republican Seward a "universal war of opinion [was] sure to come at some future time, [one] which . . . can end only in the subversion of monarchy and the establishment of republicanism on its ruins throughout the world." That conflict had not occurred during the 1820s because the Concert of European powers had other, more pressing, engagements. But the eruption of the slavery crisis in America would provide another opportunity, and even a pretext, for Old World aristocracies to strike at representative government in the New World. It would then be necessary for the United States to resurrect a dormant Monroe Doctrine and apply it with patience, firmness, and magnanimity. Seward's efforts in the Senate during the 1850s to oppose American expansionism and the misapplication of the Monroe Doctrine to British policy in the Caribbean were models of decorum and good sense.[10]

Repeatedly Seward warned Americans against a foreign policy of aggrandizement. "Adjacent states," he observed, "though of foreign habits, religion and descent, especially if they are defenseless, look with favor upon the approach of a power that will leave them in full enjoyment of the rights of nature, and at the same time that it may absorb them, will spare their corporate existence and individuality." Seward believed that the incorporation of distant societies, as already of Indian, Mexican, and Spanish territories, was inevitable. But, he insisted, "I advocate no headlong progress, counsel no precipitant movement, much less any one involving war, violence, or injustice. I would not seize with haste, and force the fruit, which ripening in time, will fall of itself into our hands. But I know, nevertheless, . . . that a continent is to be peopled, and even distant islands to be colonized by us."[11] No American, he advised, should embrace the "miserable delusion that we can safely extend empire, when we shall have become reckless of the obligations of eternal justice, and faithless to the interests of universal freedom." The ruins of past civilizations were "filled with relics and implements of human torture and bondage, showing the ignorance and barbarity of their former occupants." While Americans built their modern empire, they should take care to leave "no trace in our history, to prove that we were false to the great interests of humanity." As the world's vindicator of human rights, the United States should confine itself, unless directly attacked by an aggressor, to peaceful persuasion.[12] Seward's faith lay not in power but in the possibilities of American civilization itself.

During the winter of 1851–1852 Seward introduced resolutions in the Senate which would offer American hospitality to Louis Kossuth, Hungary's famed revolutionary leader, and condemn the brutal repression by the Russians and Austrians of the Hungarian insurrection. Whenever attempts are made "to throw off . . . despotic systems of government," said Seward, "the existing despotisms of Europe combine to repress those struggles." Americans should always "honor those who serve the cause of civil liberty through-out the world. That cause is our cause." And while nonintervention in the internal affairs of foreign nations should remain the Ameri-can credo, the citizens of the United States should always extend "hospitality to all who fly from oppression and despair." Americans, Seward warned, could not "extinguish sympathy for freedom elsewhere, without extinguishing the spirit of freedom which is the life of our own republic." The United States, he admonished, "forever must be, a living offense to . . . despotic powers everywhere." Americans could "never, by whatever humiliations, gain one friend or secure one ally in Europe or America that wears a crown." The truth was that "freedom . . . sometimes mistakes her friends; but tyranny is never deceived in her enemies."[13] The United States, in defense of its own interests and of the common interests of mankind, while habitually recognizing the sovereignty of *de facto* governments, should be "by no means indifferent when . . . a government is established against the consent of any people by usurpation or by armed intervention of foreign . . . nations." American leaders should speak out, unconcerned whether "we shall unnecessarily offend powers whom it is unwise to provoke." For it was "not enough for a nation that it has no enemies. . . . It is necessary that a state should have some friends. . . . Exemption from hatred obtained by insensibility to crime is of no value; still less is the security obtained by selfishness and isolation. Only generosity ever makes friends, and those that it does bring are grateful and enduring."[14] But generosity for Seward could embrace attitudes of tolerance and patience toward those governments whose behavior he deplored.

Seward, reflecting the spirit of revolutionary Europe no less than his own conviction that America remain a model republic, often expressed sentiments reminiscent of the Jeffersonian reac-tion to the French Revolution. But Seward, as he often reminded his listeners, would no more than his predecessors attempt to embody such notions in the ongoing foreign policies of the United States. During the Polish uprising of 1863, suppressed by Russian forces, Napoleon of France sent an appeal to the United States for support in exerting "a moral influence on the Emperor of Russia." In his response of March 11, 1863, Seward acknowledged the American interest in public order and humanity; he admitted that revolutionaries of every country had been attracted to American democratic idealism and had attempted to involve the United States in their affairs. But, Seward added, the American policy of nonintervention had remained inviolate since the time of Washington. Under no foreseeable circumstance would the United States defy its own principle of self-determination. "Our policy of non-intervention, straight, absolute, and peculiar as it may seem to other nations," he wrote, "has thus become a traditional one, which could not be abandoned without the most urgent occasion, amounting to a manifest necessity."

Seward abhorred war. He called it "the bane of republics," convinced that war, unless severely controlled, would inevitably transform them into despotisms. "A democratic government," he said, "has no adaptation to war. . . . War, however brief its duration, and however light its calamities, deranges all social industry, subverts order, and currupts public morals." The first element of the country's happiness and security, then, was peace. War, by contrast, was "the chiefest of national calamities, [and] so incongruous with the dictates of reason, so ferocious, so hazardous, and so demoralizing, that I will always counsel a trial of every other lawful and honorable remedy for injustice, before a resort to that extreme measure of redress; and, indeed, I shall never counsel it except on the ground of necessary defence."[15] No really great, enlightened nation, declared Seward, ever needed to make war as a matter of honor; for "true national honor, which feels a stain more keenly than a wound," was commensurate with "justice and good faith," and not with "enterprises which spring from a desire for glory" and material gain. The way to achieve glory was "by prosecuting beneficent designs." Nations were often debilitated by their wars; they were "seldom impoverished by their charities."[16]

Seward argued that nations were more apt to become poor and debt-ridden because of ambition, revenge, and the lust for territory than from the expenditure of energy and resources in internal improvements. "Palaces and pyramids," he contended,

the luxurious dwellings of living tyrants, and the receptacles of their worthless ashes when dead, have in every country but our own cost more than all its canals and roads. [And governments in every era have] disbursed more in a single war than was required to complete a system of improvements sufficient to perfect their union, wealth, and power, and enable them to defy invasion or aggression. Internal improvement, then, is the antagonist . . . of war. It commands the support of those who would benevolently advance the greatest happiness of the greatest number, as well as the efforts of those who would increase the national honor, elevate the national glory, and extend the sway of public virtue.[17]

Throughout the 1850s the Senate gave Seward a forum in which he could pursue his twin goals of expanding commerce and restricting slavery. Although he was no believer in a coming millenium, he cherished the hope that "as war has hitherto defaced and saddened the Atlantic world, the better passions of mankind" were beginning to develop in the aptly named Pacific theater. Peace was now to have its sway, ran Seward's prediction, and commerce would be "the great agent of this movement"—not commerce upheld by armies and navies which would in time become too costly, but peaceful worldwide trade making use of the unsurpassed forest, mineral, and agricultural resources of the United States. Commerce was the means by which the republic would advance its civilization at home and enlarge its empire abroad.[18]

First would come a federal land policy that would encourage the augmentation of American agriculture so that surpluses would be available for foreign trade.[19] Industry also Seward would stimulate with subsidies, including tariff protection. Then would come the rush of internal improvements. "Open up a highway through your country from New York to San Francisco," Seward advised. "Put your domain under cultivation, and your ten thousand wheels of manufacture in motion. Multiply your ships, and send them forth to the East. The nation that draws the most material and provisions from the earth, and fabricates the most, and sells the most of productions and fabrics to foreign nations, must be, and will be, the great power of the earth."[20] When Americans built a merchant marine sufficiently large to command the seas, they would be able to dominate "the commerce of the world, which is the empire of the world."[21] This trade was above all "to be looked for . . . on the Pacific ocean, and its islands and continents." To participate in it fully, the United States must, finally, build an isthmian canal, either through Nicaragua or Panama, preferably the latter. Only thus could America's destiny to build and control a commercial, not a territorial, empire be fully attained.[22]

II

Following the election in 1860 of the first Republican president, Abraham Lincoln, seven Southern states seceded from the Union and formed a separate slave-holding confederacy. Faced with the imminence of that irrepressible conflict which by insistent warnings he had long tried to avert, Seward feared that disunion would produce rival societies whose jealousies would sustain a perpetual civil war. Such division would invite European interference. Foreign nations, Seward predicted, would intervene "now in favor of one and then in aid of another; and thus our country . . . would . . . become the theatre of transatlantic intervention and rapacity." Seward doubted that representative government in America could survive the presence of European influence. The two distracted, beleaguered American confederacies "would sooner or later purchase tranquillity and domestic safety by the surrender of liberty, and yield themselves up to the protection of military despotism."[23]

For Seward civil war was inimical to democratic government. Why should a people use force to oppose and overthrow a government when they possessed the ballot? Seward dreaded, he said, "as in my innermost soul I abhor, civil war. I do not know what the Union would be worth if saved by the use of the sword." The most injurious trait of political rebellions, he wrote, was their "tendency to subvert the good understanding and break up the relations existing between the distracted state and friendly nations, and to involve them, sooner or later, in war." As Lincoln's newly appointed secretary of state, Seward instructed American diplomats abroad to exercise "the greatest possible diligence . . . to counteract and prevent the designs of those who would invoke foreign intervention to embarrass or overthrow the Republic." The interposition of the European powers would be fatal to his hope of a peaceful reunion when the national sentiments of North and South alike had time to exert their influence.[24]

Seward's apprehensions, both of European military incursions into Latin America and of attempts by the great powers to meddle in the internal disorders of the United States, were soon justified. He learned that Spain had sent a military expedition to retake its former Caribbean colony of Santo Domingo; that the French were sending warships to the North American coast and might attempt to invade their former colony of Haiti; that the British, French, and Russian ministers in Washington had advised their governments to grant diplomatic recognition to the nascent Southern Confederacy; and that there would probably be a punitive invasion launched by several European powers against Mexico. In addition, the British minister in Washington threatened intervention on the side of the slaveholders if the United States government should attempt to employ economic coercion against the rebellious cotton states in the form of a naval blockade of their seaports.[25]

Obviously Seward faced a formidable foreign policy crisis. He wrote his wife that he was beset with anxieties, with "dangers and breakers . . . before us." He endeavored to convince Lincoln that the emergency required immediate, decisive action by the chief executive "to rouse a vigorous . . . *spirit of independence* . . . against European intervention" in the Western Hemisphere. Lincoln, he believed, should replace traitorous or lackadaisical diplomatic and consular representatives abroad with men who would deliver categorical demands for explanations of the intentions of foreign governments regarding events in America. The leaders of those governments he would warn that "an act of recognition" would encourage the Southern insurrectionists "to attempt to establish their separation from the Union by civil war, the consequences of which would be disastrous to all the existing systems of industrial activity in Europe." There should be an energetic prosecution of a national effort to fend off foreign intervention while there was still time to do so. Lincoln's mind was fixed momentarily on political patronage. He replied that he would consider the secretary of state's suggestions, but that in doing so he desired the advice of the entire cabinet.[26]

Lincoln in the crisis rejected Seward's counsel regarding Fort Sumter and yielded to the admonitions of his postmaster general, Montgomery Blair, to "vindicate the hearty courage of the North." He ordered a naval relief expedition to sail for Charleston harbor. The result was civil war, exacerbated by the prompt secession of four border slave states and the outbreak of insurrectionary movements in three others. The more belligerent Jacksonian faction in the cabinet had prevailed. Not only had the "irrepressible conflict" taken a violent turn but also it had raised the danger that the imbroglio would involve the European nations as well. Seward set to work to ward off possible foreign intervention. He directed his

London representative to admonish the British that "if they determine to recognize the Confederate government, they may at the same time prepare to enter into alliance with the enemies of this Republic." Any country which recognized a revolutionary state "with a view to aid in effecting its sovereignty and independence," wrote Seward, "commits a great wrong against the nation whose integrity is thus invaded." Such a recognition would inevitably widen the area of war. "What part of this continent or of the adjacent islands," Seward asked, "would be expected to remain at peace?" Indeed, it was likely that "convulsions of incalculable magnitude, would threaten the stability of society throughout the world," including components of the British Empire.[27] To his envoy at Paris Seward wrote that the United States would resist any form of outside interference or influence in the war of the Southern rebellion. "Foreign intervention," he declared, "would oblige us to treat those who should yield it as allies of the insurrectionary party, and to carry on the war against them as enemies. The case would not be relieved, but, on the contrary, would only be aggravated, if several European states would combine in that intervention."[28]

Seward's warnings arrived in Europe too late to prevent precipitate action there; nor were his words at first taken seriously except as exemplifying, in the words of Lord Richard Lyons, the British minister in Washington, the secretary's total "disregard of the rights and feelings of Foreign Nations" and his lack of understanding of the importance to the Lincoln administration "of conciliating the European Powers." In mid-May, Seward learned that Great Britain and France had agreed to act together in regard to the American question. Such an arrangement was pointless unless the two great powers contemplated some form of intervention. Gestures in favor of European mediation; hints of European recognition of Confederate independence, and even threats of war to obtain Southern cotton and bring about the permanent dissolution of the American Union—all greatly depressed Seward. He wrote to his wife: "They have misunderstood things fearfully in Europe." Great Britain seemed to contemplate becoming "the ally of the traitors." And the French had already announced that they would be guided by British policy toward the United States. The American secretary of state set himself the task of preparing new instructions, bold and decisive, to meet the danger of intervention and a trans-Atlantic war.[29]

On May 21 Seward wrote Charles Francis Adams, the new

American minister in London, that American "relations in Europe have reached a crisis, in which it is necessary . . . to take a decided stand." He neither meant "to menace Great Britain nor to wound the susceptibilities of that or any other European nation." But the British foreign minister's statement that he was not unwilling to discuss American problems with accredited representatives of the Southern Confederacy, the already announced entente between the British and French governments to act together in regard to American affairs, and threats by both Lord Lyons in Washington and prominent members of the British Parliament to force open the Northern blockade of the Southern seaports in order to procure cotton for British textile factories, combined to create a situation that portended an Anglo-American war, if not an even wider one.[30] Seward warned that discussions of any kind between the Southern commissioners and the British foreign secretary were "liable to be construed as a recognition of the authority which appointed them. . . . Moreover, unofficial intercourse is useless and meaningless if it is not expected to ripen into official intercourse and direct recognition." If Lord Russell, the British foreign minister, persisted in seeing the insurrectionists, Adams was to break off diplomatic relations with the London government and await further instructions from Washington.[31]

Seward's warning continued. Any European intervention to break the federal blockade of Southern ports, he wrote, would be met militarily. If Great Britain became "the patron of privateering when aimed at our devastation" by recognizing insurgent commerce raiders as lawful belligerents and providing "them shelter from our pursuit and punishment," the United States would treat such ships as pirates and would seek an adequate and proper remedy in the law of nations which allowed claims for damages against such depredations. Any recognition of Confederate sovereignty and independence would "not pass unquestioned by the United States." Nor would the Lincoln administration fail to object to any concession of belligerent rights to the rebel government which was apt to be construed as a recognition of that government. Certainly the state department would revoke the exequaturs (the licences to function officially) of any British consuls who disowned federal authority over the entire country, North and South. For any form of British recognition would be "British intervention, to create within our territory a hostile state by overthrowing this Republic itself."[32]

Despite Seward's repeated warnings, both the British and French governments, attempting to find an opening for intervention, offered to mediate the North-South conflict. Seward had anticipated this and as early as April 22, 1861, had seized the suggestion favoring European mediation made by Governor Thomas Hicks of Maryland to declare "that no domestic contention whatever, that may arise between the parties of this Republic, ought in any case to be referred to any foreign arbitrament, least of all to the arbitrament of an European monarchy." When the British foreign minister persisted in offering mediation, Seward replied that he would never sanction any form of intervention "from any, even the most friendly, quarter." Later, to a French mediation proposal, the secretary of state responded that the Emperor Napoleon's generous offer, although greatly appreciated, could never be accepted. For no conflict resembling the American Civil War "was ever ended but by exhaustion of one or both of the parties." Moreover, wrote Seward, "the integrity of any nation is lost, and its fate becomes doubtful, whenever strange hands . . . are employed to perform the proper functions of the people, established by the organic laws of the state."[33]

By offering to guarantee the safety of British commerce with federally controlled ports in the South, and by promising prompt military action to regain control over those ports which remained in rebel hands, Seward hoped to avert a concession of belligerent status to the Confederacy by European governments. He was also prepared to offer liberal compensation to English shippers whose property should be lost as a result of depredations by rebel warships. In return, he wanted all the ports of other nations closed to Southern "pirates." But the secretary of state's efforts "to remove every cause that any foreign power could have for the recognition of the insurgents as a belligerent power" were doomed by the adamant opposition of the British minister in Washington. His paranoia reinforced by whispers from Senator Charles Sumner, whose efforts to undermine Seward (in order to obtain his office) continued intermittently for several years, Lyons sent a series of dark warnings to London that the secretary of state's overtures were really part of a scheme to provoke a war with England. On guard and sensing a trap where none existed, the British foreign minister refused to agree to a reciprocal arrangement.[34]

Another problem arose when Lyons, acting on orders from London, initiated a diplomatic negotiation, to be conducted by the British Consul at Charleston, S.C., with the authorities at Richmond. Objecting to an action that could have been the first step toward full diplomatic recognition of the insurgent government, Seward revoked the exequatur of Consul Robert Bunch. Having been discovered in their covert move to establish contact with the Confederate government, the British blustered and threatened military movements, and even talked of war. But in time they backed off and took care thereafter, with Seward's tacit consent, to transact only the most vital business with the rebel regime, cautiously and at arms length.[35] Seward believed that every communication he had sent to foreign governments demonstrated "an earnest solicitude to avoid even an appearance of menace or of want of comity towards foreign powers." In addition, he had tried diplomatic initiatives to reduce the chances of maritime incidents growing out of the American Civil War, thereby exemplifying his desire to avoid "giving any cause of offense or irritation to Great Britain." It nevertheless appeared to him that the British leaders had "been inattentative to the currents that seemed to be bringing the two countries into collision."[36]

III

Late in 1861 an Anglo-American war looked almost inevitable. The *Trent* affair was one of the most dangerous diplomatic crises in American history. It began with the forcible seizure from a British mail steamer, the *Trent*, under the orders of Captain Charles Wilkes of the *U.S.S. San Jacinto*, of two Confederate commissioners and their secretaries, bound to England and France with instructions to induce the governments of those nations to intervene in the American Civil War on the side of the South. Seward saw immediately that Captain Wilkes's act had, at the worst possible time, revived "a question [impressment] . . . which heretofore exhausting not only all forms of peaceful discussion, but also the arbitrament of war itself, [had] for more than a century alienated the two countries from each other, and perplexed with fears and apprehensions all other nations." Seward began with extreme care to defuse the *Trent* bomb. First, he wrote Adams in London that Captain Wilkes had "acted without instructions" from the United States government, which, he added, was "disposed to confer and act with earnestness" to avert conflict over the *Trent* abduction. Next he inserted in the President's annual message to Congress, which did not directly mention the *Trent* affair, an assertion that the United States intended to "commit no belligerent act not founded in strict right, as sanctioned by public law."

He confided to the French minister that he intended to use every means possible to avoid a rupture with England. Then he received from Lyons an ultimatum demanding the restoration of the four Confederate captives and an apology for their seizure within seven days, in the absence of which Lyons would close the British legation and leave the country. Knowing that the British were arming for war, Seward first persuaded Lyons to wait four days before making official delivery of the British demands, which would provide that much more time for the warlike ardor in both countries to diminish; and then he engaged himself in gathering information bearing on the subject, including legal precedents, newspaper commentaries, sworn statements by Wilkes and his officers, diplomatic dispatches, and private letters from abroad. Carefully he drew up an elaborate justification of the release of the rebel captives, basing it on traditional American principles of international law.[37]

When Lincoln's cabinet met on Christmas day to consider the British ultimatum, Seward's first task was to convince his colleagues that defiance would mean a probable war with England, regarding which not a single continental country would be in sympathy with the United States. He did this by reading dispatches and letters recently received from Europe. His next task was to change the mind of Lincoln, whose natural inclination to temporize under pressure had led him to fall in with an idea urged upon him by Senator Sumner, that an offer to arbitrate the question would prevent a break in diplomatic relations. After Seward provided evidence that arbitration, even if an unbiased umpire could be found, would be unacceptable to the British government, and after Lincoln saw that no other member of the cabinet endorsed the idea, the President yielded to what the attorney general called "the necessity of the case," and abandoned his arbitration idea.[38]

Only Seward had a concrete plan for meeting the exigency, embodied in the draft of a diplomatic note to Lyons in which he proposed "cheerfully" to release the Southern commissioners and their secretaries, on the ground that Wilkes had unintentionally violated international law in capturing them without also taking possession of their "contraband" papers and the *Trent* as well. It would be unwise, Seward told the other cabinet members and the President, "to be diverted from the cares of the Union into controversies with other powers, even if just causes for them could be found." After a second session of the cabinet on December 26, in which a few amendments were attached to Seward's paper, the members of the cabinet and the President resolved unanimously to approve it, and with it the release of the Confederate captives in time to meet the terms of the British demand. Thus was an Anglo-American war narrowly averted.[39]

IV

As the Civil War entered its second year, Seward confronted an increasing danger of European intervention, either in the form of an attempt to dictate a settlement based on disunion, or as an outright armed attack on the blockade of Southern cotton ports. While opposing a plan favored by a large majority in Congress and a majority of the cabinet to replace the Federal naval blockade with a mere edict announcing that the cotton ports were closed to foreign commerce, a step which the British minister had said his government would "deem it their duty to resist . . . by force if necessary," Seward had also to contend with a stream of objections from England that, in one place or another, the blockade itself was insufficiently tight to be respected by Her Majesty's government. Interspersed, however, among these complaints were allegations that the blockade was *too* efficient in thwarting the efforts of Lancashire textile manufacturers to obtain an adequate supply of raw cotton. Urging the cabinet to hasten military movements leading to the early capture of such Southern ports as Norfolk and New Orleans, the secretary of state continued to remind European leaders that their manufacturers would be most likely to obtain cotton when the American Union was restored. Intervention, he warned, would assure them no cotton and would deny them northern grain and markets for their manufactured goods.[40]

Dozens of American merchantmen had been destroyed on the high seas by Confederate warships built in British shipyards and kept supplied largely in British ports. Calling these abuses of neutrality "deeply injurious" to the United States, Seward issued orders to have "the legal proofs in support of a claim for indemnity . . . collected." Meanwhile he pledged to do "everything possible to prevent a ripening of these disturbances into a war upon the ocean, which would probably leave no nation free from its desolating effects."[41] The depredations continued, however, resulting from what Seward called "the indiscriminate and unlimited employment of capital, industry, and skill by British subjects, in building, arming, equipping, and sending forth ships-of-war from British ports to make war against the United States." Moreover, English seaports around the world were open "to the visits of piratical vessels," and furnished them with fuel, repair facilities, and provisions. This amounted "to a naval war waged by a portion at least of the British nation against the government and people of the United States—a war tolerated . . . by the British government." The federal government, Seward said, would defend American vessels "in our harbors and on the high seas, even if we must unhappily be precipitated, through injustice in Europe, into a foreign war."[42]

By mid-summer of 1863, Seward believed that the two English-speaking nations had reached a crisis. The United States was drifting, "notwithstanding our most earnest and vigorous resistance, towards a war with Great Britain. Our commerce on the high seas is perishing under the devastation of ships-of-war that are sent out for that purpose from British coasts, by British subjects." Fresh, "more formidable" warships, "designed even to dislodge us from the military occupation of insurgent ports and to burn and destroy our principal cities," were about to leave England. Such an assault "by British built, armed, and manned vessels," known as the Laird rams, would make "a retaliatory war inevitable." Seward pleaded with British leaders not to "let a blow fall . . . that will render peace impossible."[43] When the British government, responding at the last possible moment to Seward's remonstrances, prevented the departure of the Confederate rams, the tension eased once more. But the American secretary of state continued to insist "that the British government is justly responsible for the damages" caused by the *Alabama* and other Confederate commerce raiders built in British ship yards. Claims would be brought forward in due course, and although, Seward admitted, there was "no fair and just form of conventional arbitrament or reference to which we shall not be willing to submit them," Seward was determined that the so-called "Alabama claims," which continued to burgeon, would ultimately be satisfied.[44]

Throughout the war years, Seward denounced "the concession of belligerent rights to the insurgents" by the European powers "as unnecessary, and in effect as unfriendly, as it has since proved injurious to this country." But he also reassured foreign governments that American resentment of the naval war waged by disaffected Americans from bases in the British realm and British provinces, would neither result in "a policy of unreasonable and litigious exactions upon the British government" nor, when the

Americans had "gained the blessings of internal peace," in an "aggressive foreign war." The atonement that the United States would claim at the hands of states which unnecessarily and unkindly had lent aid and sympathy to the insurgents, he said, would be based on a policy of justice and magnanimity. Realizing "how hard it is for a state to retrace an erroneous course so long as it can be followed without immediate peril," Seward was not surprised or discouraged at the unwillingness of the European powers to recede from their untenable positions toward the dying Southern rebellion. But the "many grave claims on behalf of our citizens," he asserted, were proliferating and would be peaceably pressed until satisfied.[45]

For almost a full year following the outbreak of the Civil War, Seward insisted that American diplomats not discuss the opposing moral principles that lay at the foundation of the controversy that had shattered the Union. The subject of slavery was taboo; the Lincoln administration, as Seward later intimated, had no intention of driving millions of loyal non-abolitionist Americans into the enemy camp by imparting to a "defensive war the character of an aggressive one for the removal of slavery," although it was clear, he acknowledged, "that slavery was the real cause of the rebellion."[46] Behind the scenes, however, Seward worked diligently to undermine the hold that slavery had obtained on national life. He quietly negotiated a treaty of naval cooperation with Great Britain for the suppression of the African slave trade. (John Quincy Adams had signed a similar agreement in 1824 but the senate had rejected it.) By 1866 the slave trade had been totally eradicated as a result of the Seward-Lyons treaty of 1862. Meanwhile, Seward also initiated diplomatic relations with the Negro republic of Haiti, and he enthusiastically supported both an act of Congress abolishing slavery in the District of Columbia and the issuance of the Emancipation Proclamation, "wisely delayed until the necessity for it should become so manifest as to make it certain that, instead of dividing the loyal people of the Union into two parties, one for and the other against the prosecution of the war for the maintenance of the Union, it would be universally accepted and sustained."[47]

V

In August, 1866, Seward declared that the time had arrived to submit the Alabama claims to the British government with a request for satisfaction. British officials had argued that Her Majesty's government had been prevented by law from interfering with the support supplied by Englishmen to the Confederate naval effort. Seward retorted that "when the municipal laws of Great Britain proved in practical application to be inadequate to the emergency," a duty existed "to revise those laws," or to become liable to "render redress and indemnity." Moreover, he concluded, such "a disregard of the obligations . . . of international law, manifested by one state, so injurious to another . . . ," was sure, sooner or later, to lead to retaliation. During the recent Fenian outbreaks, sympathizers in the United States had attempted to organize auxiliary land and naval forces for invasions of Ireland and Canada, but American authorities had put "municipal laws into execution and prevented the threatened invasions." Seward could not guarantee similar behavior in the future unless the Alabama claims were "amicably and satisfactorily adjusted."[48]

For over three years Seward argued the American case so effectively in diplomatic correspondence with Great Britain that he gradually stripped away all the defenses set up by three foreign ministers and their Washington spokesmen, while—as he was also dealing with the French to move them out of Mexico—he incrementally increased the pressure for a settlement. "If delays are continued," he warned in March, 1867, the situation "may perhaps pass beyond the reach of settlement by a friendly correspondence." The ultimate result of his long campaign, especially of his careful construction of an invulnerable case for the United States, was the Treaty of Washington and the Geneva arbitration award that followed. The United States received an apology and a payment of fifteen and one-half million dollars. Never before had Great Britain been so thoroughly vanquished by peaceful diplomacy. Yet the settlement left behind no residue of rancor; indeed, the Geneva arbitration of 1872 may have been the key event in changing the Anglo-American relationship from one of traditional enmity to one of friendly, if informal, alliance.[49]

A similar attitude of studied moderation marked Seward's diplomatic campaign which produced the French withdrawal from Mexico in 1867. "Handled with masterly restraint, with a minimum of international friction, with complete diplomatic success," according to one authority, this transaction was "one of the most brilliant in the annals of our foreign policy." And even though Seward's initial objections to the annexation of San Domingo by Spain in 1861 exuded "unnecessary braggodocio," and his objections afterward to the Spanish seizure of the Chincha Islands from Peru had an especially "high tone," Spain eventually yielded to Seward's remonstrances and withdrew by mid-1865 from both places, "without manifesting any particular resentment toward the United States."[50]

Besides working to clean up the diplomatic debris left by the Civil War itself, Seward began during his last years in office to lay the foundations for a vast American commercial empire overseas. Attempting to promote the benign influence of American ideals, along with the expansion of American commerce, into foreign lands, expecially into Asia and Latin America, he insured a prominent place for himself in the record of United States foreign relations by such achievements as his negotiation in 1867 of the Alaska purchase treaty, his acquisition that same year of the Midway Islands, and his signing the following year of the Seward-Burlingame treaty which, by recognizing the territorial integrity of and the principle of equal commercial opportunity in China, anticipated John Hay's later Open Door policy. In addition, Seward strengthened the American position in Japan; laid the foundation for a settlement of the northwest boundary controversy which recognized American sovereignty over the San Juan islands; promoted the construction of the Atlantic cable; and worked for an international postal convention. So effectively did he apply pressure on the British government to recognize American naturalization, that this longstanding problem, which had been one of the causes of the War of 1812, was finally put to rest by the Protocol of 1868, confirmed by the Treaty of 1870. During Seward's tenure as secretary of state, he negotiated more treaties with foreign governments than did all of his predecessors combined.[51]

Many of Seward's ventures in pursuit of his dream of American "worldwide commercial hegemony" were not immediately crowned with success. Among these were his attempts to annex Hawaii; to open up trade with Korea; to acquire bases in Greenland, Iceland, Haiti, and San Domingo; to purchase portions of the Danish West Indies (Virgin Islands); to take possession of territory needed for the construction of an interoceanic canal through either Panama or Nicaragua; to build an intercontinental telegraph from the Mississippi River to the capital of Russia; and to procure agreement on an international gold standard and a common coinage that would facilitate the dollar becoming the basic international medium of exchange. It should be recognized, however, that Seward was handicapped first by the exigencies of the Civil War, and afterwards, during the postwar reconstruction period, as his minister in London put it, by "a fractious Senate and delirious representative chamber on one side, and a not over flexible chief on the other." It was a wonder that he accomplished as much as he did to establish so many foundations on which others later built.[52]

By 1865 Seward's prewar fame was already in eclipse. The statesman whose public addresses before 1861 had always drawn huge crowds, and who had during the 1850s commanded more space in newspapers nationally for his ideas than any other Republican, was allowed to share little of the postwar glory lavished upon the nation's uniformed warriors or upon the martyred Lincoln. When he died in 1872, following a round-the-world tour and an abortive attempt to write his autobiography, Seward's former political rivals were quick to publish memoirs, later used as "sources" by historians, which deprecated and distorted his role in history, and invented incidents—like the so-called "foreign war panacea" project of early 1861—which had no basis in reality.[53]

Seward's entire public life was spent primarily as an educator. He sought office not for power or profit, but because he could thereby obtain a forum for the widest discussion of his ideas. Always he strove to remind the American people of their heritage and to inform them about what he believed was their "mission" in the world. As a young state senator he sought to inculcate the leaders of the New York Whig Party with a desire for economic and social reform. As governor of his state, he sought to make its citizens supporters of the ideal of human betterment. As a United States senator from 1849 to 1861, believing that "to disseminate knowledge and to increase virtue" were the highest duties of statesmanship, he did his best to "maintain the principles on which the . . . preservation of . . . natural rights" rested. As secretary of state during the Civil War, he labored to preserve the Union, which carried the hopes of humanity. In his diplomatic instructions, widely published both in newspapers and in official compilations, he reminded the American people of their human rights traditions and their collective role as social reformers in a world dominated by reactionary vested interests. These missives provided the American people, as had his Senate speeches during the 1850s, with a public philosophy which enabled them to understand the need for stamina and sacrifice during the nation's most tragic war. His published statements put the Civil War in historic perspective, not only relating it to the revolutionary struggle that gave birth to the great republic, but pointing the way to an expanding world role that was to come.[54]

NOTES

1. In his well known appraisal of the office of secretary of state, Alexander De Conde ranks Seward second in performance only to John Quincy Adams. *The American Secretary of State: An Interpretation* (New York: Frederick A. Praeger, 1963), p. 171. For similar assessments, see Walter La Feber, *The New Empire: An Interpretation of American Expansion, 1860-1898* (Ithaca: Cornell University Press, 1975), p. 25; Richard W. Van Alstyne, *The Rising American Empire* (New York: W. W. Norton and Co., 1974), p. 176; Ernest N. Paolino, *The Foundations of the American Empire: William Henry Seward and U.S. Foreign Policy* (Ithaca: Cornell University Press, 1973), p. 212; and Deane and David Heller, *Paths of Diplomacy: America's Secretaries of State* (Philadelphia: J. B. Lippincott Co., 1967), p. 86.
2. Norman A. Graebner, "Northern Diplomacy and European Neutrality," *Why the North Won the Civil War*, ed. by David Donald (Baton Rouge: Louisiana State University Press, 1960), pp. 53, 72.
3. The best biography of Seward is Glyndon Van Deusen's *William Henry Seward* (New York: Oxford University Press, 1967). Important, also, is a three-volume memoir produced by his son, Frederick W. Seward, as *Autobiography of William H. Seward, From 1801 to 1834, with a Memoir of His Life, and Selections from His Letters from 1831 to 1846* (New York: D. Appleton and Co., 1877); and *Seward at Washington as Senator and Secretary of State. A Memoir of His Life with Selections from His Letters* (New York: Derby and Miller, 1891), 2 vols.
4. William H. Seward, *Life of John Quincy Adams, Sixth President of the United States* (Philadelphia: Porter and Coates, c. 1849), p. 396. Part of this book was ghost written by the Rev. John M. Austin. (*Seward at Washington*, I, 109.)
5. *The Works of William H. Seward*, ed. by George E. Baker (Boston: Houghton Mifflin and Co., 1884), III, 209, IV, 336.
6. Seward, *Works*, III, 23, 293.
7. *Ibid.*, III, 23, 196, 292-93, 468, IV, 132.
8. *Ibid.*, III, 468, 496-97, IV, 149, 152-53, 169.
9. *Ibid.*, III, 90-91.
10. *Ibid.*, III, 91, IV, 125.
11. *Ibid.*, III, 188, & IV, 167-70. The "ripe fruit" metaphor was a favorite not only of Seward (see *ibid.*, I, 273, 293), but also of John Quincy Adams. (See Van Alstyne, *Rising American Empire*, p. 148.)
12. Seward, *Works*, III, 189-90, & IV, 367, 512.
13. *Ibid.*, I, 175, 177, 184, 206.
14. *Ibid.*, I, 196, 204-205.
15. *Ibid.*, I, 202, & II, 275, & III, 267-68, 288. "Aggression," asserted Seward, . . . "is in every case weakness. Self-defense in a righteous

173

cause is the strongest attitude that an individual or a nation can have. The weakest nation may resist a powerful adversary while it occupies an attitude of self-defense." Hence powerful nations were often reluctant to launch "an unprovoked attack upon one infititely weaker than themselves." (*Ibid.*, V, 485.)

16. *Ibid.*, I, 154, 298, & II, 188. Seward opposed making war on Mexico for Texas in 1846. He called it "an unjust war—the game of . . . despots, not of democracies—and, above all, not of the democracy of the American states." He desired "no enlargement of territory," he said, "sooner than it would come if we were contented with 'a masterly inactivity.'" And in 1850 he said: "I want no more Mexican wars, no more lust of conquest, no more of seizing the unripened fruit, which if left alone, would of itself fall into our hands." (*Ibid.*, I, 293, III, 251-52, 409.)

17. *Ibid.*, III, 319.

18. *Ibid.*, I, 57, 154, 250, IV, 248.

19. In a senate speech on "The Public Domain," delivered on February 27, 1851, Seward advocated what eventually became the Homestead Act of 1862. (See *ibid.*, I, 156-71; also p. 289. for another speech urging large grants of public land to be given to foreign immigrants.)

20. *Ibid.*, III, 618.

21. Seward's references to the "empire of the seas," the "supremacy of the seas," and the "empire of the ocean" might be taken as evidence that he was an ideological precursor of Admiral Arthur T. Mahan, the great exponent of national seapower. But Seward's emphasis was upon peaceful trade, not upon the warmaking power of a mighty navy. Warships, he believed, were for protection, not for committing acts of aggression or intervention.

22. Seward, *Works*, I, 57, 250, & III, 618, & V, 33-34, 578, 590, 605.

23. *Ibid.*, IV, 651-59. Frederic Bancroft, hardly an uncritical admirer of Seward, called his senate speech of January 12, 1861, an address "as wise, as patriotic, and as important as has ever been delivered within the walls of the Capitol." *The Life of William H. Seward* (Gloucester, Mass.: Peter Smith 1967 reprint of 1889 Harper and Bros. ed.), II, 16.

24. Seward, *Works*, IV, 652, 666, 669, & V, 293, 322; Seward to all U.S. ministers, March 9, 1861, State Department records, National Archives (hereinafter "NA").

25. Norman B. Ferris, *Desperate Diplomacy: William H. Seward's Foreign Policy, 1861* (Knoxville: University of Tennessee Press, 1976), pp. 3-10.

26. *Seward at Washington*, I, p. 534; *The Collected Works of Abraham Lincoln*, ed. by Roy P. Basler (New Brunswick: Rutgers University Press, 1953), IV, 316-18. See Seward no. 2 to C. F. Adams, April 10, 1861, NA, for an elaboration of Seward's policy of "justice, forbearance, and moderation."

27. Seward no. 2 to Adams, April 10, 1861, NA.
28. Seward no. 3 to W. L. Dayton, April 22, 1861, NA.
29. Ferris, *Desperate Diplomacy,* pp. 12-13, 18-21.
30. Seward no. 10 to Adams, May 21, 1861, NA.
31. *Ibid.*
32. *Ibid.* This instruction has been cited along with Seward's "April Fool's" memorandum to Lincoln, as evidence of a "foreign war panacea policy—a scheme to provoke a trans-Atlantic conflict that would bring about the reunification of north and south in defense of the Union against European aggression. I have said on many occasions that I think the evidence for this idea, consisting largely of unsubstantiated rumors and false reports, and distorted if not totally inaccurate interpretations of the aforementioned two documents, falls apart when subjected to critical analysis and to a common sense examination of the crucial materials in their historical context. Although the "foreign war panacea" thesis, which has found its way into many textbooks, as well as into scholarly monographs, and even into *Parade* magazine, was implicitly refuted in my book *Desperate Diplomacy,* it was categorically contravened in a paper read on July 31, 1981, at that year's annual meeting of the Society for Historians of American Foreign Relations in Washington, D.C., at which time I not only traced the idea to its sources but also suggested the ignoble motives that gave it birth. An apt contemporary characterization of Seward's tenth instruction to Adams came from the historian and diplomat John Lothrop Motley, an anglophile, who nevertheless thought the document "unobjectionable in every way—dignified, reasonable, and not menacing, although very decided." *The Correspondence of John Lothrop Motley,* ed. by George W. Curtis (New York: Harper and Bros., 1900), II, 142.)
33. Seward, *Works,* V, 609; Seward no. 21 to Adams, June 19, 1861, & Seward nos. 13 & 234 to Dayton, June 8, 1861 & October 8, 1862, all NA.
34. Ferris, *Desperate Diplomacy,* pp. 24-31, 37, 47-48, 55-63, 77-83; Norman B. Ferris, "Transatlantic Misunderstanding: William Henry Seward and the Declaration of Paris Negotiation of 1861," *Rank and File: Civil War essays in Honor of Bell Irvin Wiley,* ed. by James I. Robertson, Jr., and Richard M. McMurry (San Rafael, Calif.: Presidio Press, 1976), pp. 55-78.
35. Ferris, *Desperate Diplomacy,* pp. 74, 80, 97-116, 196, 200.
36. Seward no. 19 to Dayton, June 17, 1861, & Seward no. 136 to Adams, November 30, 1861, both NA.
37. Seward to Lyons, December 26, 1861, & Seward no. 136 to Adams, November 30, 1861, both NA; Norman B. Ferris, *The Trent Affair: A Diplomatic Crisis* (Knoxville: University of Tennessee Press, 1977), pp. 130-33, 177.

38. Ferris, *Trent Affair,* pp. 177-86.
39. *Ibid.,* pp. 183-87.
40. Ferris, *Desperate Diplomacy,* pp. 87-90. The excellent treatment of Anglo-American relations during the Civil War era contained in Brian Jenkins's *Britain and the War for the Union* (Montreal: McGill—Queen's University Press, 1974, 1980), 2 vols., has in my opinion eclipsed the classic studies by Ephriam D. Adams, *Great Britain and the American Civil War* (New York, Russell & Russell, 1925), 2 vols., and Frank L. Owsley, *King Cotton Diplomacy: Foreign Relations of the Confederate States of America* (Chicago: University of Chicago Press, 1959).
41. Seward nos. 373 & 385 to Adams, October 20 & November 3, 1862, & Seward no. 58 to T. Corwin, October 21, 1862, all NA.
42. Seward no. 651 to Adams, July 11, 1863, NA.
43. Seward nos. 669 & 700 to Adams, July 30 & September 5, 1863, both NA.
44. Seward nos. 729 & 730 to Adams, October 5 & 6, 1863, both NA.
45. Seward nos. 104 & 406 to Dayton, January 23, 1862 & September 26, 1863, and Seward nos. 209 & 235 to Adams, March 15 & April 19, 1862, & Seward no. 26 to B. Wood, February 24, 1862, & Seward circular instruction no. 39, August 12, 1863, all NA.
46. Seward nos. 2 & 1174 to Adams, April 10, 1861 & December 5, 1864, and Seward no. 3 to Dayton, April 22, 1861, all NA.
47. Seward, *Works,* V, 10-12; Seward circular instruction to legations and consulates dtd. September 22, 1862, NA.
48. Seward, *Works,* V, 443, 446-47, 450-52; Brian Jenkins, *Fenians and Anglo-American Relations during Reconstruction* (Ithaca: Cornall University Press, 1969), pp. 137-50.
49. Seward, *Works,* V, 475-76; La Feber, *New Empire,* p. 313 Of course Seward had been gone from the state department for more than two years when the Treaty of Washington went into effect. But without his idea of "due diligence" and his laborious groundwork there could have been no such diplomatic triumph as the Geneva arbitration "Alabama claims" award. The Johnson-Clarendon convention, providing for the mutual settlement of Anglo-American claims since 1853, was not signed until two months before Seward left office, and was a clumsy effort which the senate overwhelmingly rejected, while Seward made no effort to save it. Largely derogatory toward Seward is the discussion in Adrian Cook, *The Alabama Claims: American Politics and Anglo-American Relations, 1865-1872* (Ithaca: Cornell University Press, 1975), pp. 29-72.
50. Dexter Perkins, *A History of the Monroe Doctrine* (Boston: Little, Brown and Co., 1963), pp. 123, 132, 135, 144-47.
51. Although the relevant literature is replete with references to these accomplishments, most writers deal with them meagerly and do not

treat them in the context of Seward's overall thought. Frederick Merk, for example, hardly mentions Seward's ideas in his *Manifest Destiny and Mission in American History: A Reinterpretation* (New York: Vintage Books, 1966). Calling Seward "the central figure of nineteenth-century American imperialism," Richard Van Alstyne confines his references to that gentleman to less than two pages of his *Rising American Empire.* Other historians of American expansionism, while devoting considerable space to Seward, appear dubious about some of his postwar projects. See, for example, the references to "the ebullient Seward," who in pursuing his "pipedreams," is described as "blissfully ignoring . . . harsh realities" in Paul S. Holbo, *Tarnished Expansion: The Alaska Scandal, the Press, and Congress, 1867-1871* (Knoxville: University of Tennessee Press, 1983), p. 14.

52. Paolino, *Foundations,* pp. 25, 210; Charles F. Adams, "Diary," April 11, 1867, microfilm ed., Massachusetts Historical Society.

53. For example, Gideon Welles, *Lincoln and Seward* (New York: Sheldon and Co., 1874).

54. Seward, *Works,* IV, 128-31, 180-81; Walter G. Sharrow, "William Henry Seward: A Study in Nineteenth Century Politics and Nationalism, 1855-1861," Ph.D. dissertation, University of Rochester, 1965, p. 41.